THE SERMON ON THE MOUNT
and Its Meaning for Today

The
SERMON
ON THE MOUNT
and Its Meaning for Today

ERNEST TRICE THOMPSON

John Knox Press
RICHMOND, VIRGINIA

ALETHEIA Paperbacks now available
   for your individual or group study:

An Adventure in Love (Christian Family Living)
   by W. Taliaferro Thompson.

Adventures in Parenthood by W. Taliaferro Thompson.

A Call to Faith (Christian Beliefs) by Rachel Henderlite.

The Gospel According to Mark and Its Meaning for Today
   by Ernest Trice Thompson.

In the Beginning GOD (Meaning of Genesis I-XI)
   by William M. Logan.

The Nature and Mission of the Church by Donald G. Miller.

Out of the Whirlwind (Study of the Book of Job)
   by William B. Ward.

Reasons for Our Faith by Henry T. Close.

The Sermon on the Mount and Its Meaning for Today
   by Ernest Trice Thompson.

The Story of the Reformation by William Stevenson.

Understanding the Books of the New Testament
   edited by Patrick H. Carmichael.

Understanding the Books of the Old Testament
   edited by Patrick H. Carmichael.

We Believe (Study of the Apostles' Creed)
   by Henry Wade DuBose.

Library of Congress Catalog Card Number: 53-11761

Fifth printing, 1964

Copyright 1946, By John Knox Press
Revised edition © M. E. Bratcher 1961
Printed in the United States of America
9729 (20) D. 6324

TO MY MOTHER

*from whom came
my earliest and most abiding knowledge
of the Christian way of life*

Contents

Many Christians believe that Jesus' teachings,

particularly those included in the Sermon on the Mount,

present beautiful ideals which cannot possibly be realized

in real life.

The writer believes that they present a practicable way of life

not only for individuals but also for society,

a way to peace and happiness in this world

as well as in the world to come,

and that they were never more necessary than now.

The Historical Background

In this brief series of studies we shall consider the Sermon on the Mount and its message for today, but to catch the full implications of this message we must study it in connection with its historical background.

THE ROMAN QUESTION

The people to whom Jesus' words were originally spoken were subject to the power of Rome, but they looked forward eagerly to deliverance and to the re-establishment of the Jewish nation as an independent kingdom.

Rome had a genius for government, and her rule brought many advantages to the Jews. Nevertheless Rome did not rule Palestine primarily for Palestine's good, but for its own good. In other words, to put it bluntly, Palestine was exploited for the benefit of the Romans, especially for the ruling class of Rome.

Take taxes, for example. The Jews were a poor people; their country lacked natural resources and was greatly overpopulated, yet it has been estimated that the taxes paid by the Jews amounted to one third of their total income. We all hate to pay taxes, no matter how large our means or how great the need, even when they are imposed by our own representatives in the state legislature or in Congress. But the Jews were a subject people, forced to pay taxes to conquerors whom they hated and despised. To make it worse, they were a proud people, a people who remembered the glorious days of the Maccabees, when they had fought against great odds and won their independence from the successors of Alexander the Great. They were convinced, moreover, that they were the Chosen People, the descendants of Abraham and Isaac and Jacob, the heirs of the promises made to them by God; it was intolerable that they should be trampled under the feet of the Gentile dogs.

Every once in a while their feelings would break out in some overt act. Four times, for example, in Jesus' own lifetime there were armed revolts against the power of Rome. The most spectacular of these revolts came when Jesus was a boy, about ten years old. It centered in Sepphoris, which was the largest city in Galilee, the second largest city in Palestine, and just three miles from Nazareth. Sepphoris was an important military post where Herod the Great had stored a large amount of arms and provisions. After his death a revolutionary leader named Judas equipped his followers with weapons from the royal palace in Sepphoris and made this region the center of his operations. The revolt was finally crushed by the Romans, who proceeded to destroy the city and to raze it and hundreds of lesser towns to the ground. Two thousand Jews were crucified and left hanging on stakes with arms outstretched, to rot, as a grisly warning to the people, a horrible example of what happened to those who dared to rebel against the power of Rome. The rest of the population, including the women and the children (thirty thousand in all), were sold into slavery.

This was the most important revolt against Rome in Jesus' day, but there were others. (Cf. Acts 5:36-37.) In fact, not a year passed without blood being shed by incipient revolutionists. Included in this number, no doubt, were the Galileans whose blood Pilate mingled with their sacrifices. (Luke 13:1.) Barabbas, whom the Jerusalem populace finally chose in preference to Jesus, was one of a group who had made insurrection and in the insurrection had committed murder. (Mark 15:7.) We cannot fully appreciate Jesus' message, we cannot really understand the development of his ministry or the opposition it aroused, unless we remember that the Jews were a subject people, seething with bitterness and resentment against the Romans, and that an explosion was likely to occur at any moment. The great question in Palestine in Jesus' day, a question which no public teacher could evade, was the Roman question—what ought to be done about Rome.

THE FOUR ANSWERS

When Jesus came into Galilee proclaiming his good news, there were four answers being given to that question. To put it more exactly, there were four parties with four different programs. We find substantially the same programs appearing and reappearing under different circumstances to the present day. They represent four different attitudes, four very popular attitudes, all of them contrary to the spirit of Jesus.

One party was that of the Zealots. They were an armed revolutionary band, relying on the dagger and the sword, waiting for the proper moment to strike against Rome. Some students think that this party was organized immediately after the fall of Sepphoris. The Romans had thought that the terrible reprisals they exacted would break the spirit of the Jews and prevent similar outbreaks in the future. Instead it inflamed the hatred of the populace and intensified their determination to break the Roman yoke. The Zealots were growing steadily all during the ministry of Jesus. They appealed especially to young men who craved action and to the common people, artisans and peasants, who had little to lose but their lives. Their influence continued to increase until finally, in A.D. 66, they instigated the revolt against Rome which ended, as Jesus had predicted, in the destruction of Jerusalem and in the collapse of the Jewish nation. The way of the Zealots was the way of force.

At the opposite pole from the Zealots were the Essenes. To them the situation in Palestine seemed hopeless. There was nothing they could do to rescue the nation from its degradation, so their minds turned in on themselves. They became ascetics and quietists. They refrained from marriage and withdrew from the ordinary life of the community. Many formed communities of their own in the wilderness. They lived lives that were personally irreproachable, but which did nothing to solve the pressing problems of the day. The way of the Essenes was the way of flight.

The third group differed considerably from the other two. They were concerned primarily with their own material advancement. They were opportunists who accepted the Roman yoke as inevitable and made terms, personally advantageous to themselves, with the conquerors.

In the north, in Galilee, members of this group were the Herodians. They said in effect, "In times like these it is every man for himself and the devil take the hindermost." So they got good jobs under Herod, lined their pockets, and preyed on the populace. In the south in Judea, representatives of this point of view were the Sadducees. They were the priestly aristocrats, the political and economic rulers of the nation, who accepted the Roman authority in order that they might maintain their profitable perquisites and prerogatives. Herodians and Sadducees differed in many things but were agreed in their determination to maintain the *status quo,* which worked to their own personal advantage. Both were quick to oppose any man or any movement which threatened in any way their privileged position under the Romans. The way of the Herodians and the Sadducees was the way of compromise.

The fourth party was that of the Pharisees. They were as religious as the Essenes and as patriotic as the Zealots. But unlike the former they did not withdraw from the common life, and unlike the latter they opposed the use of the sword. They adopted a pacifist attitude, however, not because they were pacifists in principle, but merely because "they knew that resistance was a physical impossibility and only invited complete destruction and devastation. They did not love Rome because they could not fight; they hated her the more. Their nonresistance was with a glowing eye and a heart full of hate, but with an arm that did not dare to strike."[1] The Pharisees said, in effect, "This is a desperate situation and we must look to God for help. He can save us from our predicament and he is the only one who can. Some day he will intervene miraculously from heaven and set up his Kingdom here on earth. All we can do is to fulfill the conditions which are required for God's intervention. If we keep the law given us by Moses and the traditions of our fathers (i.e., their traditional interpretations of the Mosaic Law), then some day, in his own good pleasure, God will intervene from heaven, punish our enemies, and establish his kingdom." To the Pharisees this faith seemed grounded in Scripture. Promises such as those found in Deuteronomy 28:1-19 were interpreted literally. Some of the rabbis taught that if the nation kept the Law perfectly "from one Sabbath to the next" God would move immediately to fulfill the promises made to their fathers.

We cannot understand the insistence of the Pharisees on every detail of the Law, their scorn of the common people who were unable or unwilling to keep the multitude of its exactions, their bitter opposition to Jesus for disregarding the traditions of the Fathers, unless we keep this fact in mind—obedience to the Law in all of its detail was necessary that the Jews might maintain their racial identity and preserve their religious heritage, and also that the way might be prepared for God's intervention, deliverance from the Romans, and establishment of the Kingdom of God.

The Pharisees were the popular religious leaders. Their insistence on the rigid observance of the Law together with the traditions of the Fathers separated the Jews from their neighbors and tended to separate the Pharisees from their fellow Jews. It incited hatred and contempt for all non-Jews, who were ceremonially unclean, and scorn and contempt not only for publicans who had sold out to Rome but also for sinners, including those who were grossly delinquent and those who were merely indifferent to the ritual and ceremonial claims of the Law. The religion of the Pharisees intensified, therefore, the racial intolerance of the Jew; it increased the nation's hatred against the Romans, and as Jesus pointed out during his last week in Jerusalem it played inevitably into the hands of the Zealots.

And so it happened. A generation after Jesus' death, the Zealots pushed the nation into war with Rome. Jerusalem fell, after one of the most terrible sieges in history, and the Jewish nation was finally destroyed.

The way of the Pharisees was the way of devotion toward God divorced from love toward man (i.e., toward man as man),

of scrupulous attention to religious practices and ceremonial observances, which obscured or minimized man's responsibility toward his fellow man. Jesus described their failure (the danger
which comes to churchmen in every age) in unforgettable words,
"Woe to you, scribes and Pharisees, hypocrites! for you tithe mint
and dill and cummin, and have neglected the weightier matters
of the law, justice and mercy and faith." (Matthew 23:23.)

THE COMMON HOPE

To understand the fundamental message of Jesus we need to
keep in mind not only these four groups with their four programs
but also the common people and their eager expectancy for the
future. The hopes of the populace centered about two things—
first, the Kingdom of God, and second, the coming of the Messiah.

The Kingdom of God meant at least two things to the Jews—
the reign of God and the blessings of God. First, it meant the
reign of God—not his reign in heaven, but his reign on earth;
not the reign of God over individuals merely, but also the reign
of God over the nation. Second, it meant the divine blessings
which individuals and society would enjoy when the reign of God
had become a fact.

These blessings fell into five different categories: (1) Political.
The Jews would be freed from the might of Rome, and the empire of David and Solomon would be re-established. Non-Jews
would be subjects or proselyted citizens. "Of a kingdom in any
other sense," says Shailer Mathews, "there is no trace, either in
the apocalyptic literature or in popular expectations"[2] (cf. Amos
9:11-12; Psalm 72:8-11; Luke 1:68-71); (2) Economic. The fields
would bring forth plentifully, and there would be abundance of
food for all (cf. Amos 9:13-14; Psalm 72:16; Luke 1:53); (3) Social.
Justice would be established in the nation and the rich would
no longer be able to take advantage of the poor, nor the strong of
the weak (cf. Psalm 72:1-4; Luke 1:51-53); (4) International. Nations would beat their swords into plowshares and their spears
into pruning hooks, neither would they learn war any more (cf.

Isaiah 2:4; Micah 4:1-4; Psalm 72:7); (5) Religious. God would write his law upon the hearts of men and all men would come to know God, from the least even unto the greatest (cf. Jeremiah 31:33-34; Luke 1:74-75).

All five of these goals would be realized when God's reign was established on earth. Some in Jesus' day emphasized certain of these blessings more than others, but all, singly or together, played their part in the common hope. They were present even in the most pious circles, groups in which the Christian movement had its cradle. (Cf. Luke 1:51-55, 68-79.) And that is significant, for these same elements persist in our own dream of the future. We want our own nation to be free and independent and powerful in the affairs of the world; we want economic prosperity, not simply for the few but also for the many; we want justice, especially for the poor and the oppressed; we long and pray for peace on earth, good will among men; and last, but by no means least, we desire a genuine revival of religion which shall write God's law on the hearts of men and which shall give a vital and satisfactory knowledge of God to all mankind.

The Jews agreed that this new society could be established only with the advent of the Messiah—a leader anointed and equipped by God for this purpose. Some expected this Messiah to be a military and political leader, especially equipped by God for the work of deliverance through the sword. He would be a mighty conqueror like David, but greater than David, great David's greater Son. Others expected the Messiah to be a purely heavenly being whom God would supernaturally send in his own time, one like the Son of Man whom Daniel had predicted would come riding on the clouds of heaven. But all agreed that the chief function of the Messiah would be the overthrow of the oppressors, the crushing of the ungodly powers which held the Chosen People in subjection. And there was a general feeling that the coming of the Messiah was imminent. This expectancy was greatly heightened by the powerful preaching of John the Baptist.

GOOD NEWS ABOUT GOD

This, briefly, was the situation when Jesus came into Galilee, preaching good news about God,* and saying, "The time is fulfilled, and the kingdom of God is at hand; repent, and believe in the gospel [good news]." (Mark 1:15.) Mark gives here a summary of the early preaching of Jesus. Other elements were added later, but they all grew out of this fundamental proclamation.

Jesus began proclaiming good news about God. This good news about God contained many items which we cannot now discuss, but it was based on the idea that God is our Father. "Pray . . . like this: Our Father who art in heaven." (Matthew 6:9.) "If you then, who are evil, know how to give good gifts to your children, how much more will your Father who is in heaven give good things to those who ask him?" (Matthew 7:11.)

The Jews believed that God was their Father, but for all practical purposes he was Father only of the Jews. The Pharisees believed he was their Father, but acted as though he were Father only of those who observed the Mosaic Law. "This crowd who do not know the law," they said, "are accursed." (John 7:49.) Jesus taught that God is the Father of all men. And this doctrine of the Fatherhood of God carries with it as an inevitable corollary the brotherhood of man. Jesus, of course, did not teach that all men actually lived as sons of God; some were in effect sons of the Devil, but even they were prodigal sons, who might some day come to themselves and say, "I will arise and go to my father." (Luke 15:11-32.) He did not mean that all men were actually brothers, but that all men were potentially brothers, that they would become brothers as they entered the Kingdom and accepted God's will for their lives.

Jesus came preaching good news about God, and this good news included the idea that God is our Father and that all men are or ought to be our brethren. These twin truths have been like

---

* The King James Version reads "the gospel of the kingdom of God." Versions based on older and better manuscripts read "the gospel of God." This may be translated, "good news from God" or "good news about God." Both ideas no doubt are included.

stars, inspiring much that is best in our civilization. They have been denied in our own century by Nazis who affirmed a doctrine of blood and race and soil. They have been practically denied in our own land by men who believe that they belong to the master race because their skin is white. But the doctrine that all men are the sons of God and therefore potentially brothers is a fundamental truth of Christianity and a lodestar which must be followed if civilization is to advance.

Jesus came proclaiming good news about God and saying, *"The time is fulfilled, and the kingdom of God is at hand."* What did he mean by the Kingdom of God? Many answers have been given to that question. To the ordinary Christian it means being saved and going to heaven. To some it means the millennium. To some, the visible church; to others, the invisible church. To still others, the life of God in the soul of man. What, then, did it mean to Jesus? There is only one way to answer the question. We must go back to the ideas of Jesus' contemporaries, to the hopes which he knew he would arouse, and then note the modifications of the popular hope which he introduced. If Jesus did not take the popular view of the Kingdom as his starting point, then there was no justification for his announcement; it was positively misleading to proclaim that the Kingdom of God was at hand. When we approach it in this way, certain things become clear.

1. For Jesus, as for his contemporaries, the Kingdom of God meant the reign of God. It meant the reign of God over the lives of individuals and society in this world as well as in the world to come. In speaking of the Kingdom, Jesus sometimes refers to the reign of God in the world which is to come. More often, however, he refers to the reign of God in this present world—as in the Lord's Prayer, "Thy kingdom come, Thy will be done, On earth as it is in heaven."

2. For Jesus as for his contemporaries the Kingdom of God meant the blessings of God—blessings which the individual and society would enjoy when the reign of God became a fact. For him these blessings were primarily spiritual: deliverance from anxiety, fear, and sin; fellowship with God, leading to love, joy,

peace, and all the blessings of eternal life. But material blessings were not excluded. "Blessed are you poor," he said, as reported by Luke, "for yours is the kingdom of God. Blessed are you that hunger now, for you shall be satisfied." (Luke 6:20-21.) "Seek first his kingdom and his righteousness," we read in Matthew 6:33; "and all these things [food and clothing] shall be yours as well."

3. For Jesus the Kingdom was not a Jewish but a universal hope. "I tell you, many will come from east and west, and sit at table with Abraham, Isaac, and Jacob, in the kingdom of heaven." (Matthew 8:11.)

4. Jesus repudiated the idea of bloodshed and violence as a means of ushering in the Kingdom. "You have heard that it was said, 'An eye for an eye, and a tooth for a tooth.' But I say to you, Do not resist one who is evil. But if any one strikes you on the right cheek, turn to him the other also . . . You have heard that it was said, 'You shalt love your neighbor and hate your enemy.' But I say to you, Love your enemies and pray for those who persecute you." (Matthew 5:38-39, 43-44.) This does not mean that Jesus was an absolute pacifist, nor that his ideals leave no place for force. We shall consider the implications of these verses a little later. It is evident, however, that Jesus did not think that the Kingdom could be established by violence.

5. Jesus taught that the Kingdom of God would come by organic growth as well as by divine intervention. It would come, he taught, through the sowing of the seed in the heart of man, first the blade, then the ear, and then the full grain in the ear; like a grain of mustard seed which grows into a tree; like leaven which gradually permeates the entire mass of dough; and then, in the end, the harvest, including the final separation of good and evil.

6. Jesus taught that the Kingdom of God was a present reality and not merely a future hope. That indeed was the very heart of his message. Mark says that Jesus came into Galilee preaching good news about God and saying, "The time is fulfilled, and the kingdom of God is at hand." (1:15.) He meant that the Kingdom of God is here now at this very moment, and that the bless-

ings of God are available now for individuals and for society in proportion as they accept God's will for their lives.

This is clearly implied by the Beatitudes—"Blessed are the poor in spirit, for theirs is the kingdom of heaven." It is embodied in his parables: The Kingdom of God is like a grain of mustard seed; like leaven; like a merchant in search of fine pearls, who having found one pearl of great value, went and sold all that he had and bought it. It is definitely taught by Jesus on his final trip to Jerusalem. The Pharisees asked him when the Kingdom of God would come. He replied: "The kingdom of God is not coming with signs to be observed; nor will they say, 'Lo, here it is!' or 'There!' for behold, the kingdom of God is in the midst of you." (Luke 17:20-21.)

Of course there is a sense in which the Kingdom of God will come in the future. We pray for the consummation of the Kingdom, the time when God's reign will become absolute in all the earth. Nonetheless, Jesus' fundamental and basic message is this: The Kingdom of God is at your very door. Its blessings are available now for the individual and for society in proportion as they accept God's will as revealed through me.

Jesus came into Galilee preaching good news about God and saying, "The time is fulfilled, and the kingdom of God is at hand: *repent . . ."*

The average man thinks that repentance means sorrow for sin. It does mean that. There can be no repentance without sorrow for misused opportunities, for the good that we have left undone, and for the wrong we have done to ourselves, to our neighbors, and to God. But the Greek word translated "repent" goes deeper than that; it means to change our mind, to change our attitude toward life, to change our way of living.

Jesus came into Galilee telling men the good news about God —that God was their Father and the Father of all men; and that God's blessings are available now for those who will accept his will for their lives. To secure these blessings, he says, men must repent, change their minds, change their attitude toward life, change their way of living.

He was talking to Zealots, men who put their reliance in the dagger and the sword, and who believed that the Kingdom of God could be established by force. He said to them, Change your minds, change your attitude, change your way of living. He was talking to Essenes, men whose personal lives were beyond reproach, but who turned away from the needs of their times to exclusive thought of themselves. He said to them, Change your minds, change your attitude, change your way of living. He was talking to Herodians, who thought only about lining their own pockets and who wanted to hold on to their jobs at any cost. He said to them, Change your minds, change your attitude, change your way of living. He was talking to Sadducees, aristocrats, successful businessmen, rich people, the political and economic leaders of Judea, men who thought more of their privileges than of their obligations, and he said to them, Change your minds, change your attitude, change your way of living. He was talking to Pharisees, professional religionists, men who were tremendously concerned about the proper observance of the Sabbath, and who tithed the very produce of their gardens, but who despised the masses of the people and who put religious forms above human needs, and he said to them, Change your minds, change your attitude, change your way of living. He was talking to all men who sought their own way rather than the way of God, to all prodigals who had wandered away from the Father, and he said to them, Change your minds, change your attitude, change your way of living.

He was talking to Zealots and Essenes and Herodians and Sadducees and Pharisees and to their spiritual descendants in our own time—men who believe that the ideal society can be established by force; men who are concerned about their own personal salvation but who ignore the great social problems of the day; men whose prime concern is the maintenance of their own privileged position or the lining of their own pocketbooks; men whose religion exhausts itself in private devotions and public observances and who forget the need for justice and mercy in the social and economic life—to all men who seek their own will rather than God's will. He said to them and he says to us, Repent, change your minds, change your attitude, change your way of living—and believe in the good news.

What good news? It came to include other elements, essential elements regarding Jesus' death, vital elements regarding Jesus' person, but the good news was first of all the good news that God is our Father, not only our Father but the Father of all men, men of every race and class and condition. It was good news that the Kingdom of God is right here at our very doors, and that the blessings of God are available now for individuals and for society in proportion as they accept God's will as revealed through Jesus Christ.

What does it mean to believe in the good news? It means to believe that Jesus was wounded for our transgressions and bruised for our iniquities, that upon him was the chastisement that made us whole, and that with his stripes we are healed. (See Isaiah 53:5.) It means to believe that he rose from the dead, and that he will come again to judge the world at the last day. But it means also to believe that God is our Father and the Father of all men, rich and poor, black and white, Japanese and Chinese, Russians, British, and Americans, and that the blessings of God are available for us as individuals, for our city, our state, our nation, and all nations, so far—but only so far—as we conform our lives to his requirements.

It means to live each day as though God were our Father, to trust him when the way is dark, to seek first his Kingdom and his righteousness. It means to live each day as though all men are now or may become brothers in Christ.

Men are longing today for the golden age, when we shall have prosperity and justice and peace and brotherhood and genuine fellowship with God. Some men postpone their hopes to another world. Some scan the heavens or search the pages of Scripture for times and seasons which Jesus said it was not for us to know. (Acts 1:7.) Other men are looking for some leader, some panacea, that will deliver us from our present evil situation. And we need leaders, wise statesmen who can lead us at least in the direction of the promised land. But we must not forget this fundamental message of Jesus, that the Kingdom of God exists now and that the blessings of God are available for individuals and for society in proportion as they accept God's will for their lives.

> The world planners gather.
> The young men mixed red blood with blue water
> And windy sands covered shattered helmets.
> The old men confer with figures
> And refashion their empires.
> They seek a solution; they have it,
> And they know it not.
>
> Once when the world was younger
> Some nineteen hundred years,
> A quiet man walked the Judean hills
> And along Galilee's shore,
> Then men left their nets.
> And he spoke to the people
> On a mountain with loaves and fishes,
> And he entered the city on a burro,
> And they hailed him emperor—
> And they nailed him to a cross.
> "The Kingdom of God is among you."
> They worshipped his teaching
> But were afraid to live it.
>
> The world planners gather,
> They seek a solution; they have it,
> And they know it not.[3]

The clearest presentation of Jesus' teaching regarding the Kingdom—what God requires of those who enter the Kingdom and what blessings they may expect to enjoy—is found in Matthem 5—7, those familiar words that we refer to as the Sermon on the Mount.

We read

> 23 And he went about all Galilee, teaching in their synagogues and preaching the gospel of the kingdom and healing every disease and every infirmity among the people. 24 So his fame

spread throughout all Syria, and they brought him all the sick, those afflicted with various diseases and pains, demoniacs, epileptics, and paralytics, and he healed them. [25] And great crowds followed him from Galilee and the Decap'olis and Jerusalem and Judea and from beyond the Jordan.

5 Seeing the crowds, he went up on the mountain, and when he sat down his disciples came to him. [2] And he opened his mouth and taught them. (Matthew 4:23—5:2.)

As Dr. Goudge points out: "The Sermon is not addressed primarily to the multitudes with the view of winning them for the Kingdom (4:17, 23), but is an instruction given to 'his disciples' who have already accepted the call. Yet it is given in the hearing of the people, for those who have 'ears to hear.' They too may perchance be awakened to repentance and faith."[4]

Just when this instruction was given to his disciples we cannot say; if the sermon in Matthew is to be identified with the somewhat similar sermon in Luke, it was six months, perhaps, after he had come into Galilee and just after he had chosen the twelve disciples who were to form the nucleus of his church.

Scholars generally agree that Matthew, following, as usual, the topical rather than the chronological order, has brought in teachings delivered by Jesus on other occasions as well. Whether or not this is the case, the sermon, or lesson rather, as we have it, is a unit.

It falls easily and naturally into three major divisions: The Citizens of the Kingdom; The Righteousness of the Kingdom; and The Summons to the Kingdom.

I

The Citizens of the Kingdom
Matthew 5:1-16

THEIR CHARACTERISTICS AND BLESSINGS

Matthew 5:1-12

5 Seeing the crowds, he went up on the mountain, and when he sat down his disciples came to him. 2 And he opened his mouth and taught them, saying:

3 "Blessed are the poor in spirit, for theirs is the kingdom of heaven.

4 "Blessed are those who mourn, for they shall be comforted.

5 "Blessed are the meek, for they shall inherit the earth.

6 "Blessed are those who hunger and thirst for righteousness, for they shall be satisfied.

7 "Blessed are the merciful, for they shall obtain mercy.

8 "Blessed are the pure in heart, for they shall see God.

9 "Blessed are the peacemakers, for they shall be called sons of God.

10 "Blessed are those who are persecuted for righteousness' sake, for theirs is the kingdom of heaven.

11 "Blessed are you when men revile you and persecute you and utter all kinds of evil against you falsely on my account. 12 Rejoice and be glad, for your reward is great in heaven, for so men persecuted the prophets who were before you."

Jesus begins by speaking of the blessedness of those who are members of the Kingdom. Blessed are the poor in spirit. Blessed are those who mourn. Blessed are the meek. Blessed . . . blessed . . . blessed—over and over he repeats the word, as though he would impress that thought first of all upon their minds. What does it mean? Some translate, "to be congratulated." The poor in spirit are to be congratulated, for theirs is the Kingdom of heaven. Others prefer the word "happy." It includes that notion, certainly; the words might very well be translated, "Oh, the happiness of." But the word goes deeper and describes a state of the soul that is far more enduring than "happiness" as we ordinarily understand it, an emotion which lives only on the surface and comes and goes as our temporary mood or changing circumstances may determine. It means true, abiding happiness, full of the greatest possible happiness, possessing the highest felicity of the soul. After all, no word is so adequate as the familiar word "blessed."

In using this word Jesus strikes an answering echo in the hearts of us all. We all want to be happy. So true is this that many philosophers have held that happiness is the *summum bonum,* that is, the highest good in life. Most of us will not admit that this is so, and yet there is no goal in life which we desire to reach unless it does bring contentment. Wisdom, business success, the accumulation of wealth, professional skill, patriotic duty, service in the Kingdom of God—all of these things we seek because we think that in securing or in rendering them we shall find peace for our souls.

The only real question we face in this connection is, How may happiness be secured and how may it be retained? To this question many answers have been returned; a thousand formulas have been devised whereby this universal desire of the human heart may be achieved. In the Beatitudes we have Jesus' answer to the question—his recipe for true, abiding happiness.

As we ponder his words, it becomes plain that in Jesus' estimation true abiding happiness (i.e., blessedness) depends on inward condition rather than on outward circumstance.[5]

We are apt to think that happiness depends on the possession of material goods, but Jesus says, "Blessed are you poor." (See Luke 6:20, 24.)

We are apt to think that happiness depends on the absence of disappointment and sorrow and pain, or upon the positive enjoyment of pleasure, but Jesus says, "Blessed are those who mourn." (Compare Luke 6:21, 25.)

We are apt to think that happiness depends on the possession of friends or upon success or prestige in the estimation of the world, but Jesus says, "Blessed are you when men revile you and persecute you and utter all kinds of evil against you." (See also Luke 6:22, 26.)

"Blessed are you poor," says Jesus.

We are inclined to think that happiness depends on the possession of material goods—that we would be happy if we had a new car, a better home, a larger income, or the means to indulge all our desires. No doubt these things would bring us joy—at least for a while. And they ought to bring us joy. Jesus was no ascetic. He came eating and drinking. His enemies called him a winebibber and a glutton. Paul said, "All things are yours." (1 Corinthians 3:21.) There are a thousand things in life that bring us happiness, and that ought to bring us happiness. God wants us to enjoy the simplest things of his bounty.

But these things do not guarantee happiness. Sometimes we walk or drive through the streets of some fine residential suburb. We see the light streaming from the homes and we stop and wonder if there is happiness there. We know wealth is there, and success in the business world, and standing in the social realm. But we are just as likely to find happiness in the humblest home in the city as we are in the finest home in the finest residential section. All of us know men and women who have money, business success, position in the social world, all the things for which the world seems to be striving with such feverish haste and anxiety—everything save one, and that is happiness. And when we read history, we find that literature is full of the sighings of successful men over the disappointment that their success has brought to them. When the prize is won, it ceases to charm. What seems like fruit in the distance crunches in the mouth like ashes.

Yes, it is true, as every great seer has pointed out—true, abiding happiness does not depend on the possession of material goods.

But Jesus goes further. He says, *"Blessed are those who mourn."*

This does not mean that in Jesus' view it is better to weep than it is to laugh. Neither does it mean that all those who mourn are blessed. There are many men and women in the world who are nursing old wounds and hugging old sorrows to their breasts and whose lives will be embittered to the end.

"Blessed are those who mourn," says Jesus, "for they shall be comforted." The English word *comfort* comes from two Latin words *con fortis,* meaning "with strength." The Greek words on which our English translation of the beatitude is based also includes the idea of strength. Comforted and strengthened, accordingly, convey the idea of the beatitude better than the single word *comfort.*

Some are comforted and strengthened in the midst of their sorrows, and all may be. Such is the meaning of Jesus' words. No man is truly blessed unless he is able to meet sorrow, to overcome sorrow, and to find comfort and strength in the midst of his sorrow. In the world you are sure to meet with hardship, grief, and pain, Jesus says in effect. Blessed are those who are comforted, who know the secret of peace, consolation, and fortitude.

In the same way Jesus says, *"Blessed are you when men revile you and persecute you and utter all kinds of evil against you."*

He does not mean that it is better to have enemies than friends. He does mean that true happiness does not depend on our friends, and that it cannot be destroyed by our enemies. Most of us regard our friends as our dearest possession, and we hope to carry them with us throughout life. But there are times when friends fail us and when those whom we have benefited turn against us. There are times when a man must be willing to face criticism, unpopularity, persecution, and even death. The man who is really blessed is the man who is able to meet unfriendliness, misunderstanding, ridicule, persecution, and, when necessary, death itself with untroubled spirit.

Not only Jesus, but life itself indicates that true, abiding happiness is dependent on inward condition and not on outward circumstances.

Some of those inward characteristics which guarantee true and abiding happiness are indicated in the Beatitudes.

Thus Jesus says, *"Blessed are the poor in spirit, for theirs is the kingdom of heaven."*

Many young people, and some older ones too, misunderstand this beatitude. They think that the poor in spirit are the poor-spirited, those who are lacking in energy, in enthusiasm, in life. This is an unfortunate conception. The Greek phrase describes those who are conscious of their spiritual poverty. Goodspeed translates, "Blessed are those who feel their spiritual need, for the Kingdom of Heaven belongs to them!"

The Kingdom of heaven, which is Matthew's usual phrase for the Kingdom of God, is the realm in which God reigns, the realm in which God's blessings are enjoyed in this life as well as the life to come.

The man who enjoys these blessings is the man who is conscious of his spiritual need. Perhaps this comes first among the beatitudes because such awareness of need is the root of all Christian witness, the condition of all further progress in the spiritual realm. The man who is intellectually satisfied will never achieve intellectual mastery. The man who is spiritually satisfied will never know the spiritual mastery which alone can guarantee happiness in all the walks of life. The man who feels his spiritual need and who uses those means of grace which enable him to grow in spiritual stature has found the roadway to true and abiding happiness—the roadway to the Kingdom of heaven.

Perhaps the reason we are not any happier than we are is that we have been so busy with the good things of life that we have neglected the best things of life; so concerned with material things that we have neglected the nurture of our souls. We do not feel our spiritual needs; therefore, we do not use as we should the means of grace which have been put at our disposal and which enable us to grow in fellowship with God.

Jesus says, "Blessed are the poor in spirit, for theirs is the kingdom of heaven." He says also, *"Blessed are the meek, for they shall inherit the earth."*

This phrase strikes strangely on the minds of many a conventional Christian. They think that what Jesus meant to say, or what he ought to have said, was, Blessed are the meek for they shall go to heaven. But that is not what Jesus said. He said, Blessed are the meek, for they shall inherit the earth. We need to awaken to the truth that Jesus had his eyes on this life, that his gospel is a way of living here and now, that it opens to us a way of happiness in this world, as well as in the world to come.

It is clear, however, that Jesus does not refer in this beatitude to real estate or to material possessions—unless, as some think, he means that it is the meek who will in the end quite literally inherit the earth, after all others, because of their lack of meekness, have squandered their patrimony and destroyed themselves.

The practical question, as it comes to us, is this: How can we make the most of the passing days—their opportunities, obligations, and tasks? How can we enjoy to the full the life which God has given us—nature and its bounty, our homes, our friends, our work, our play? In Jesus' words, how can we "inherit the earth"— the earth which God has created for our use and stocked so bounteously for our enjoyment? Jesus says, "Blessed are the meek, for *they* shall inherit the earth.

Someone has said that the meek may inherit the earth, but the strong take it away from them. But that is to misunderstand the meaning of the biblical term. Unfortunately, it has come to be accepted as a synonym for weakness. The meek man is regarded as a timid, shrinking soul, a sort of human door mat who allows other men to trample upon him almost at will.

But that is not what the Bible means by meekness. Two men stand out in its pages as possessing this quality above all others. One is Moses, who is termed the meekest of men. The other is Jesus, who said, "I am meek and lowly in heart." (Matthew 11:29, K.J.V.) Both of them were strong, virile men who led hosts of followers, awed mobs, faced tyrants, braved dangers and death. They were not weak in any sense.

The Bible uses the word meekness in two different senses— sometimes to indicate meekness toward man and sometimes to

indicate meekness toward God. Meekness toward God, as one can
easily discern through a careful study of the Psalms, means submission to God, acceptance of his will for our lives. Meekness
in relation to men means gentleness, consideration, courtesy, in
all the relations of life. A meek man is a man who has that
"gentleness which wedded to strength makes a man"—he is a
gentle-man, or as we would say, a gentleman.

Such a man does not always win material reward. He may
indeed be very poor in real estate. But he is the man who will get
the most out of life—he will, in Jesus' phrase, inherit the earth.

Yet the promise cannot be confined to the here and now. To
inherit the earth meant to the Israelite the promised land, i.e.,
Palestine. In Psalm 37 the phrase is used figuratively of entering
into the possession of the divine blessing. In the New Testament
our inheritance is eternal life, salvation, or more frequently the
Kingdom of God. Each of these terms has a reference to two
worlds: this world and the world to come. The meek man is
blessed; he has discovered the secret of true and abiding happiness because he has entered into his inheritance which he shall
enjoy more fully in eternity.

Perhaps the reason we are not more happy than we are is because we have not really accepted God's will for our lives, because we have not been more thoughtful and considerate of those
with whom we come in contact.

Jesus said, "Blessed are the meek, for they shall inherit the
earth." He also said, *"Blessed are those who hunger and thirst for
righteousness, for they shall be satisfied."*

Who are the truly happy people? Those who get what they
want, many will reply. There is some truth in the reply, but it is
not all true. Many about us are unhappy because they have not
been able to obtain the objects or the ends on which they had
set their hearts. There are many others, however, who are unhappy because having secured their heart's desire they find that
it does not bring the happiness for which they had hoped. As
Oscar Wilde phrased it, "In this world there are only two

tragedies. One is not getting what one wants, and the other is getting it. The last is much the worst, the last is a real tragedy." (From *Lady Windermere's Fan*.)

The object of one's desire, to ensure happiness, must have at least two characteristics: first, it must be obtainable; second, it must give reasonable promise of bringing satisfaction when it is obtained. Is there anything which has these two characteristics? Jesus says there is. "Blessed are those who hunger and thirst for righteousness, for they shall be satisfied."

Some will reply that they have known good people who were not very happy. No doubt that is true. I have known them too. But if a man is hungry, he knows that he is in need and nothing will satisfy him but food; if a man is thirsty, he knows that his throat is parched and nothing will satisfy him but drink. Jesus does not say blessed is the man who thinks he is good, or who is good in the estimation of his fellow men; he says, "Blessed are those who hunger and thirst for righteousness," with all the intensity of a hungry man who longs for food, or of a thirsty man who is famished for drink. Jesus says, "Blessed are those who hunger and thirst for *righteousness*," which includes both personal and civic righteousness.

Many have failed to find the happiness they seek because they have been satisfied with conventional standards of morality, or because they have lowered their ideals to meet the ideals of the world, or because they have allowed selfishness or sin to separate them from their fellow men and therefore from God, or because they have sought justice only for themselves. None of us will find the happiness which we seek until our conscience is at rest, until we have sought and found the righteousness of God which is available to us through faith in Jesus Christ.

Jesus says, "Blessed are those who hunger and thirst for righteousness, for they shall be *satisfied*." There are various kinds of hunger and various kinds of satisfaction. Some hungers by their very nature can never be satisfied; others, like the hunger for food, find temporary satisfaction, but the hunger returns and must find renewed satisfaction. There are still other hungers whose satisfaction brings satiety or even revulsion.

But there are also hungers whose satisfaction brings lasting joy and at the same time a deeper hunger and capacity for a fuller satisfaction and a greater joy. In this category fall the hunger for the good, the beautiful, and the true, and also the hunger for the highest type of love. The successful searcher after truth is rewarded by a satisfaction which can never be taken from him, and with it comes ability to apprehend further truth, which in turn brings greater joy. So it is with the artist who hungers and thirsts after beauty; with the lover who gives himself unreservedly to his beloved; and so it is with the man who hungers and thirsts after righteousness. Satisfaction of this hunger not only brings abiding peace, but also the longing and the capacity for a higher righteousness. The final satisfaction of this hunger, as is also true of the other hungers of this type, comes in the future life, when, as John says, "We shall be like him, for we shall see him as he is." (1 John 3:2.)

Jesus says, "Blessed are those who hunger and thirst after righteousness." He also says, *"Blessed are the merciful, for they shall obtain mercy."*

The late Thomas Lomax Hunter, a popular columnist in the Richmond (Virginia) *Times-Dispatch,* once wrote, "If ever I enjoy the constitutional right of trial by jury, I trust that it will not be a jury of good men. Good men, in the sense in which the word is generally understood, have so little sympathy with bad men; are so seldom kind. Being good men themselves, they think the law should make everybody else good. In a long experience as a lawyer I have always struck off good men from the jury when I had the opportunity. Good men are convictors." Mr. Hunter exaggerated, but all of us recognize the type that he had in mind, men who are not only righteous, but also self-righteous; men who finding it easy to be righteous themselves are harsh in their judgments of those who do not measure up to their own standards. It is no accident, I think, that Jesus' beatitude regarding the righteous is followed immediately by another, "Blessed are the merciful, for they shall obtain mercy."

All along life's way we need mercy from our fellow men. We all make mistakes, say foolish words, do the wrong thing, do the right thing in the wrong way or at the wrong time. We continually blunder, even when we do not deliberately choose wrong. "One of the surest conditions of real joy is then that I shall find mercy, kind judgment, generous treatment, from my friends and companions. And if I need this at the hands of men, how much more at the hands of God!"[6] I cannot live in any sort of peace and happiness unless "His mercy is ever around me, forgiving me, understanding me, helping me to try again. Yes, 'blessed are they that obtain mercy,' as they move through this intricate business, this complex network of personal relationships, which we call life. To obtain kindly judgment from God and man is a rare and sure condition of true happiness."[7]

Who is most likely to find this mercy from God and from man which is one of the essentials of happiness? The merciful, Jesus replies, and our common sense renders the same verdict. "Men will deal generously with all sorts of sinners, will pardon grave offenses, will overlook serious faults; but scarcely anyone will show mercy to one who is himself hard, ungracious, unforgiving, and mean."[8] And what about God? Jesus has not left us in any doubt about the matter. The one character he "adjudged hopeless is the unloving, the ungenerous, the proud, the self-righteous, the unmerciful."[9]

Perhaps the reason we are no happier than we are is that we have been too harsh, too unsympathetic in our judgment of our fellow men, too unwilling to overlook trivial errors or small peccadilloes, too unwilling to pardon grave offenses. Or it may be that we have not sought, and therefore have not found, the mercy of God which is available to us in Jesus Christ.

Jesus said, "Blessed are the merciful, for they shall obtain mercy." He also said, *"Blessed are the pure in heart, for they shall see God."*

There are many sights which bring us joy. A beautiful sunset, a lofty mountain range, the skyline of a modern city, or some rare work of art. Not all of us are able to travel and to see the treasures of art or the wonders of nature. "But there is one object of vision more satisfying than any other, the contemplation of which brings the deepest and highest joy man can know"— and that is the vision of God. "How could one fail to be happy, if he could *see* God? Back of all the problems of life, back of evil and distress, through all the clouds that darken our sky, through all our questioning and doubts, to see God, the Father; to know that 'behind the dim unknown standeth God within the shadow, keeping watch above His own,' would bring such peace of mind, such confidence, that one could not help being happy."[10]

How can we attain this satisfying vision of God. Jesus tells us, "Blessed are the pure in heart, for they shall see God." When we read these words it seems "as if someone pointed to the top of a steep, lofty, inaccessible mountain, and said, 'There you will find what you seek.' We look up in awe, and look down in shame, and murmur, 'It is high, I cannot attain unto it.' "[11]

Yet we know that Jesus is right. Impurity, insincerity, dishonesty in thought, word, or deed, does obscure the vision of God. It is true that none of us can be absolutely pure, but we can want to be, we can try to be, we can earnestly pray to be, and in proportion as we succeed, I suspect that we shall find that promised vision of God.

It is not the mystic's vision that Jesus had in mind. As Dr. George A. Buttrick says: "More likely he meant that the pure in heart see God in the world about them when others are blind; that the pure in heart are aware of the movements of the Divine Will in their lives even in the midst of pain, when others are rebellious or despairing; that the pure in heart have by intuition the leading of God's spirit when others feel bereft; that the pure in heart have times of vision when earth and flesh fall away . . . and that at last they shall veritably see God in the consummation of the kingdom."[12]

The first six beatitudes all emphasize one essential fact—true, abiding happiness depends on inward condition rather than on outward circumstances. The last two beatitudes emphasize another important truth which must be put alongside the first—that true, abiding happiness depends on participation in some activity in accordance with God's great purposes for the universe.

This thought is also expressed in the beatitude which Paul quotes in his address to the elders of the church in Ephesus (Acts 20:35): "Remembering the words of the Lord Jesus, how he said, '*It is more blessed to give than to receive.*'" This translation does not bring out the full force of the original. It suggests that the donor is more blessed, or happier, than the recipient of a gift. This may very well be true, but Jesus' words go much further. Moffatt brings out the meaning when he translates, "To give is happier than to get."

Jesus does not deny that men find satisfaction— and legitimate satisfaction—in getting. There is pleasure in getting books, friends, professional skill, money, fame, or power. But one finds more happiness, more true, abiding happiness, in giving than he does in getting. The older we become the more we realize that this is true. The things which bring the most enduring satisfaction are not the things which we have gotten for ourselves, but the things which we have given to our children, to our friends, to our church, to our community, to our nation, and to our God.

This truth is given a special application in the seventh beatitude—"*Blessed are the peacemakers, for they shall be called sons of God.*" To be a peacemaker means something more than being peaceable or amiable or kindly in one's own personal relationships. It means to make peace between man and man, or between man and God.

It is a difficult business to be a peacemaker in this modern world, and sometimes a very dangerous one. It is not strange that Jesus followed this beatitude with one about being persecuted for righteousness' sake. One who would bring about peace in the world must be willing to toil laboriously, to live dangerously, to fight sacrificially, to endure pain and misunderstanding, and, it may be, to face even death itself. Jesus is the Prince of Peace, and the way he took, and the way he told us we must take, is the way of the Cross.

And yet one of the surest ways of being happy is to do what we can to bring peace to individuals who are estranged, to bring peace in the social world, in the industrial world, in the economic world, in the international world, to make peace between God and man. It is only as we get away from our own narrow interests and take some part in causes which are working for human betterment that we begin to feel that we are fellow workers with God in the great causes he has at heart, and that we begin to find true and abiding happiness.

Perhaps the reason we are not more happy is that our lives are too narrow or too selfish—we are troublemakers instead of peacemakers—we are too little concerned about others, too much concerned about self.

In the next beatitude Jesus goes a step further: *"Blessed are those who are persecuted for righteousness' sake . . . Blessed are you when men revile you and persecute you and utter all kinds of evil against you falsely on my account."*

Jesus does not mean to say that it is better to be persecuted than to be free from persecution. The point is that living in a world where righteousness, especially the righteousness of Christ, must make its way against opposition, "the one who will endure hardship rather than weakly abandon his convictions is happier than the one who will yield his convictions rather than suffer."[13] No man can be truly happy unless he has the courage of his convictions, unless there are some things for which, if need be, he is willing to suffer. The man who is willing to abandon his convictions because it is expedient or popular has introduced into his mental and spiritual life a source of discord that is bound sooner or later to destroy the very happiness that it seemed for a moment to promote.

A good illustration of Jesus' meaning comes from the experience of Dr. Turner who was pastor of the American Church in Berlin for some years before the outbreak of World War II. Shortly before he left Germany, he went to call on Pastor Heinrich Niemoeller, the father of Dr. Martin Niemoeller, who spent so many months in a German concentration camp. The old man, then 83 years of age, preached for Dr. Turner the famous sermon that he was preaching all over Germany. It seems strange that he himself was not put in a concentration camp, yet he was unmolested, presumably because of his venerable age. The sermon was based on Jeremiah 29:11-14, and emphasized the fact that everything depends on the outcome—God in the outcome—"not what the Christian's condition is now, but where he ends up." The old man told the story of how Napoleon's mother entered her son's tent at a time when he was at the height of his power. "Son," she said, "you are Napoleon, the world conqueror. But you have an anxious mother who asks where you will end up, what will your outcome be?" "And Father Niemoeller looked pointedly at me," said Dr. Turner, "to see whether I was bringing the application up to date. Then he continued to its end the sermon on the God who is the Alpha and the Omega, the beginning and the end of human history." The time came for Dr. Turner to leave. "As we stood at the door," he said, "Grandmother Niemoeller held my left hand in her two hands. The grandfather of Martin's seven children patted my right hand and then put one hand on my shoulder. 'When you go back to America,' he said slowly, 'do not let anyone pity the father and mother of Martin Niemoeller. Only pity any follower of Christ who does not know the joy that is set before those who endure the cross despising the shame. Yes, it is a terrible thing to have a son in a concentration camp,' the aged saint concluded. 'Paula here and I know that. But there would be something more terrible for us: if God had needed a faithful martyr, and our Martin had been unwilling.' "

There could be no better illustration of Jesus' beatitude.

We repeat. That blessedness which the world cannot give and which the world cannot take away depends on inward condition rather than on outward circumstances. It comes from participation in some unselfish activity; it is found by the peacemakers, by those who are willing to suffer for righteousness' sake, and above all for Christ's sake. God pity any follower of Christ who, living in such times as these, does not know the joy that is set before those who endure the cross, despising the shame.

THEIR INFLUENCE AND RESPONSIBILITY

Matthew 5:13-16

13 "You are the salt of the earth; but if salt has lost its taste, how shall its saltness be restored? It is no longer good for anything except to be thrown out and trodden under foot by men.

14 "You are the light of the world. A city set on a hill cannot be hid. 15 Nor do men light a lamp and put it under a bushel, but on a stand, and it gives light to all in the house. 16 Let your light so shine before men, that they may see your good works and give glory to your Father who is in heaven."

After having described the characteristics and blessings of the members of the Kingdom, Jesus proceeds to speak of their influence and responsibility. They have the influence of which he is about to speak because they possess the characteristics of which he has spoken. The privileges or blessings which they enjoy are balanced by their responsibilities. Jesus describes this influence and this responsibility by the use of two figures, salt and light, both of which are indispensable and both of which are irreplaceable; two figures which indicate the unique position his disciples are to occupy in the world.

"You are the salt of the earth . . . You are the light of the world." The reference is not to their opinions, nor to their beliefs, but to themselves. You—not the political and economic and religious leaders of the nation, but you—common people, men and women in every walk of life, who have found your way into the Kingdom. "You *are* the salt of the earth . . . You *are* the light of the world." Jesus does not say that they ought to be, or that they will be in some later age or in some future life, but that they are now, when so many problems perplex and when so many dangers threaten. "You are the salt of the *earth* . . . You are the light of the *world*." Some people say that Jesus was interested only in individual souls; that he had no concern for, and therefore that his church has no direct concern for, the social order. This opinion does not square with Jesus' words here or elsewhere. Jesus was concerned with the individual, as we must be also, because the world cannot be changed unless individuals are changed, but he also taught that changed individuals must set out to change "the earth" and "the world."

He was speaking to a little group of men in an obscure corner of the Roman Empire. To speak of this insignificant company as the salt of the *earth,* as the light of the *world,* would have been laughable in any other. "But in that little company, he saw the womb of the future. He saw the ever-increasing host of faithful men and women who would gather around him as these had done. He saw his own sweetness and light carried by renewed lives innumerable into the dark and putrid places of humanity. He saw himself magnified and reproduced everywhere. He saw morning breaking for all in the world in the lamp which he had kindled. He spoke not to these twelve men alone. He spoke to his own through all generations. The words are in our ears. They speak to our hearts and consciences. If we believe in him they belong to us. If we love him, they are true to us. 'Ye are the salt of the earth; ye are the light of the world!'" (Greenhough.)

The first figure describes the duty, the danger, and the possible doom of Christians in their relation to society.

First, the duty—*"You are the salt of the earth."* One function of salt is to season. Salt gives food taste and saves it from being flat and insipid. As a child once explained, "Salt is what makes food taste bad when you don't put it in." The function of the Christian is to season life so that men everywhere shall find it purer, lovelier, more enjoyable, cleaner, for the saving salt of their character. The Christian virtues really make life worth living.

Some think that religion, especially the Puritan conception of Christianity, is a kill-joy. And some Christians have indeed made the mistake of opposing simple joys that are perfectly innocent in themselves. On the other hand there are some sensual pleasures, some social amusements, some attractive vices, that finally destroy happiness and are inconsistent with true Christian living. But the religion of Jesus does not make life insipid; it makes it pleasant, rich, and satisfying, not for some men only, but for all men everywhere. Life without the Christian virtues, as we have come to see more clearly in recent years, becomes a life that is not worth living, that is intolerably cruel, and that will in the end destroy civilization itself. As followers of Christ, it is our duty to make life wholesome and zestful, not only for our children, but also for children in the slums; not only for American children, but also for children in Europe, Asia, and Africa. "You are the salt of the earth," Jesus said.

Salt not only seasons, it also preserves. It destroys germs and prevents decay. That function was more in evidence in Jesus' day, when there was no artificial ice and no electric refrigeration, than it is in our own.

Agents of decay are working today to destroy the character of individuals; to undermine the foundations of our family life, our economic life, our political life; and to spoil international understanding. We have seen the corruption these germs have produced in other lands and in other times. Unless checked, they will bring civilization once more to the verge of collapse. Christians and the Christian virtues alone can preserve society from decay. Military strength is not enough; organization of the world for peace is not enough. Germs which destroy the health of humanity must be destroyed; society must be made wholesome and pleasant for all.

As the great ecumenical conference at Oxford said in 1937: "Political remedies are not enough. All law, international as well as national, must be based on a common ethos, that is, a common foundation of moral convictions. In the creation of such a common foundation in moral convictions, the Church, as a suprarational society with a profound sense of the historical realities and of the worth of human personality, has a great contribution to make." This last is a typical British understatement. As a matter of fact, the church has not only a great but an indispensable contributon to make.

The glory of the twentieth century, someone has said, is that all the world has been made a neighborhood; the tragedy of the twentieth century is that the world has been made a neighborhood before people have learned to be neighborly. There is only one force in the modern world which can teach men to be neighborly—not communism or fascism, not education or science or government, certainly not the fear of the hydrogen bomb, not even religion, but only the religion of our Lord and Saviour Jesus Christ.

"As an ecclesiastical corporation the church has often failed, but there have been in all ages, even in the worst times, some whose home influence and whose obscure lives have been preserving the world from corruption, for towards that end every devout heart and every pure life constantly tends. This work of theirs does not require publicity or any great capacity. Salt does its work silently by simply being in contact with that which needs its conserving power, and all that is required of it is that it should keep its own peculiar saltiness, and should remain in contact with what it preserves." (Rowland.)

But there is a danger that the salt will lose its taste. Chemically this is not possible, but practically it often happened in Palestine that the salt was mixed with dirt and became therefore quite worthless. So the Christian often does not affect his environment but is instead affected by his environment; he does not transform the world but is conformed to the world. Salt that had become corrupt was good neither for the land nor for the dunghill; it could neither fertilize nor purify; and as a troublesome, harmful thing it would be cast into the roadway, where it could not do much harm, there to be trodden under foot by men.

This was the doom which Jesus warned might befall the church if it failed to fulfill its function in the world. And it has happened over and over again as Jesus predicted. Many have turned against the church, not because it was salt, but because in their esti-

mation it had become a narcotic; not because it destroyed the
agents of decay, but because it taught men to accept injustice
in the world and to live in hopes of the world to come—"pie in
the sky by and by." For some, we are forced to admit, religion
has become an opiate; but those who follow Christ's way of life
are the salt of the earth—and the light of the world.

The second figure describes the nature of the Christian's mission, its importance, and its fulfillment.

1. Its nature. *"You are the light of the world."* The world,
Jesus intimates, is now enveloped in darkness. Certainly that
is true in our own day. We did not realize it so clearly a generation ago, but we recognize it now. Somehow we have missed the
way; and science, education, industry, military victory, even
world organization, do not guarantee that we shall find it. *"You
are the light of the world,"* said Jesus.

What a lamp is to a home—to the one-roomed cottage of the
Oriental peasant—that the Christian is to the world. He, and he
alone, has that truth about God and man which can dispel the
darkness of the world's ignorance and sin and can lighten the
way that leads to peace and security for all mankind.

2. Its importance. *"A city set on a hill cannot be hid. Nor
do men light a lamp and put it under a bushel, but on a stand,
and it gives light to all in the house."* So the Christian's life cannot be concealed, whether he fails or whether he succeeds,
whether he be little or whether he be great. A Christian who
falls into sin attracts more attention than a non-Christian; a follower of Christ who shuts his heart against human need arouses
hatred against the cause of Christ. On the other hand, every true
Christian helps to lighten the way. As Dr. Merrill points out:
"Christianity has spread through the shining lights, Brooks,
Drummond, Moody, Wesley, Luther, Wiclif, Saint Francis, and a
host of others, who shine like great beacons that cannot be hid.
But it has spread at least as much, probably far more, through
the simple candlelight in innumerable homes. Not every Christian can build a city on a hill; but every Christian can light a

candle,"[14] that in his corner of the earth, at least, the darkness shall not fall.

3. Its fulfillment. How can a Christian fulfill his mission? Not mainly or chiefly by the words which he speaks (though Jesus did not underestimate the power of words), but by the life which he lives. *"Let your light so shine before men, that they may see your good works and give glory to your Father who is in heaven."* As Elton Trueblood has said, "Christianity lives or dies not by what goes on in the churches, but by what goes on outside of them." We reveal God most clearly in the world, we spread the light most effectively, when we live lives that reflect the spirit of Christ and that will lead men to glorify the God and Father of us all.

And that brings us to the second section of the Sermon on the Mount—the section that deals more fully with the Christian way of life.

II
The Righteousness of the Kingdom
Matthew 5:17—7:12

This division of the Sermon on the Mount, dealing with "the righteousness" which is expected of the members of the Kingdom, falls into four natural subdivisions: (1) Its nature, 5:17-48—key verse, 5:20; (2) its observance, 6:1-18—key verse, 6:1; (3) its value, 6:19-34—key verse, 6:33, and (4) its gaining, 7:1-12.

THE RIGHTEOUSNESS OF THE KINGDOM—
ITS NATURE
Matthew 5:17-48

1. THE GENERAL PRINCIPLE. Matthew 5:17-20

> 17 "Think not that I have come to abolish the law and the prophets; I have come not to abolish them but to fulfill them. 18 For truly, I say to you, till heaven and earth pass away, not an iota, not a dot, will pass from the law until all is accomplished. 19 Whoever then relaxes one of the least of these commandments and teaches men so, shall be called least in the kingdom of heaven; but he who does them and teaches them shall be called great in the kingdom of heaven. 20 For I tell you, unless your righteousness exceeds that of the scribes and Pharisees, you will never enter the kingdom of heaven."

To understand this paragraph we need to recall that the religious leaders of Israel actually thought that Jesus was irreligious. He did not act like other pious folk. He claimed prerogatives which it seemed to them belonged only to God (Mark 2:7); he associated with religious and social outcasts (Mark 2:14-17); he disregarded many of their sacred traditions, including those which centered about the Sabbath (Mark 2:18; 2:23—3:6). It seemed to the Pharisees that he was a dangerous revolutionary who was undermining the foundations of their faith.

Jesus assures his disciples that he came not to abolish but to fulfill their traditional religion. He is not speaking here of fulfilling the types and prophecies of the Old Testament (though he did fulfill such types and prophecies), but, as the context plainly reveals, of filling full the ethical and moral teaching of the Law and the Prophets (i. e., the Old Testament), of giving their incomplete teaching and their imperfect ideals their complete and perfect expression. As Theodore H. Robinson puts it, he came "to make complete, to perfect, to emend, to give the temporary thing, with its numerous occasional details, an eternal validity. The Law had been an interim expedient, the best that could be devised until the fulness of time, for the securing of certain ends. But under the regime of Jesus these ends can be still better secured, and the Law, though superseded as the final authority, will be fulfilled, completed, absorbed into a higher rule of life."[15]

This statement throws light on the Old Testament revelation. In Jesus' estimation it was neither perfect nor final; it reached its culmination and found its completion in him. Christians, then, must read their Old Testament in the light of that fuller revelation which has been given in Jesus Christ. Any moral ideal, any conception of God, in the Old Testament which falls below the revelation given by Jesus must be regarded as inadequate and incomplete.

The statement in verse 17 is further explained in verses 18, 19, and 20. Verse 18 emphasizes that he did not come to abolish ancient truth. It has been interpreted in various ways, but probably means that not one bit of the Law shall pass away until it has served its purpose, until all things be accomplished by it that God has meant for it to accomplish. As someone has put it: "Whatever does pass away does not pass by destruction [or abolition] but by fulfillment—i.e., the evolution of its hidden life, as the bud passes into the rose. The bud is there no longer, but it is not destroyed, it is fulfilled in the rose."

This leads Jesus, in verse 19, to sound a "warning to anyone who would assume a hostile or trifling attitude toward great moral verities. Whoever believes himself to be above the law will find in the last great day that he is least in the kingdom of heaven. But whoever will accept these imperishable principles and build his life thereon, the same shall be called great in the kingdom of heaven."[16] The order of the clauses is significant: "whoever then relaxes . . . and teaches . . . he who does . . . and teaches them." One does not ordinarily teach men to disregard the moral verities until he has broken with them in his own life; the inculcation of moral truth has little value unless the teacher himself practices the moral ideal which he professes.

Verse 20 explains why it was necessary for Jesus to perfect the Old Testament teachings. "For," says he, "unless your righteousness exceeds that of the scribes and Pharisees (the most religious people of that day), you will never enter the kingdom of heaven." It is difficult for us to conceive the full impact of these words for those who originally heard them. The Pharisees were men who bent every effort to keep the Law in its smallest details; the scribes were the scholars of the party and gave themselves to the understanding and interpretation of the Law. "In the eyes of their own generation the two classes had attained the very summit of that goodness which lay in keeping the law, and it was the occupation of a lifetime to reach and maintain their standards." Yet Jesus tells his disciples that such goodness is insufficient, and that in the new community, goodness must excel that of the most highly revered religious leaders of the day.

2. SPECIFIC APPLICATIONS. Matthew 5:21-48

Having enunciated the general principle that he came to complete the revelation of the Old Testament, Jesus proceeded to illustrate in specific ways how the righteousness of the Kingdom exceeded the righteousness of the scribes and Pharisees. In general we may say that Jesus makes righteousness more real and vital, a matter of the heart and not merely the observance of formal statutes.

Anger and Contempt. Matthew 5:21-26

> 21 "You have heard that it was said to the men of old, 'You shall not kill; and whoever kills shall be liable to judgment.' 22 But I say to you that every one who is angry with his brother shall be liable to judgment; whoever insults his brother shall be liable to the council, and whoever says, 'You fool!' shall be liable to the hell of fire. 23 So if you are offering your gift at the altar, and there remember that your brother has something against you, 24 leave your gift there before the altar and go; first be reconciled to your brother, and then come and offer your gift. 25 Make friends quickly with your accuser, while you are going with him to court, lest your accuser hand you over to the judge, and the judge to the guard, and you be put in prison; 26 truly, I say to you, you will never get out till you have paid the last penny."

The Old Testament prohibited murder. Jesus, tracing the sin back to the heart, says that the man "who is angry with his brother shall be liable to judgment . . ." In the King James Version there is a clause added which makes the verse read, "whosoever is angry with his brother *without a cause* shall be in danger of the judgment." This clause, "without a cause," is omitted in the Revised Standard Version because it is not present in the older and best manuscripts. Evidently it was added by some scribe who found the original statement too difficult without some qualification. But Jesus said, *"Every one who is angry with his brother shall be liable to judgment."*

Did Jesus mean to say that it is always wrong to be angry— that we sin whenever we lose our tempers? We know that he could not have meant that, for he himself became angry at times. Thus in Mark 3:5 we read that Jesus "looked around at them with anger, grieved at their hardness of heart." And Paul writes in Ephesians 4:26, "Be angry, but do not sin," which indicates that in his judgment there are times when it is sin to be angry and times when it is not. As a matter of fact, anger is one of the sinews of the soul. If we can look out upon the world today at the various signs of man's inhumanity to his fellow man and not become tremendously indignant, then there is something wrong with our moral fiber. The trouble with most of us is that we become angry at the wrong things. We lose our tempers when something interferes with our own ease and pleasure. So far as we know Jesus never became angry when things went wrong with him; but his anger flared time and time again at the wrong done to others.

Jesus does not say that anger is always a sin, or that it always subjects us to adverse judgment. Rather, as translated in the Revised Standard Version it renders us liable to judgment. The King James Version and the American Standard Version bring out the force of the statement by using the word *danger* in their translation: "Every one who is angry with his brother shall be in *danger* of the judgment." (A.S.V.)

Anger is dangerous for the individual. It works up steam. It sets up physiological reactions that release energy, which is probably its biological function in life. It enables the organism to meet some sudden emergency that threatens its existence. But unfortunately, anger which releases energy also destroys judgment. It throws us off our mental balance. As a result we say and do things when we are angry that we would never say or do in moments of calmer judgment. And sometimes the things we say when we are angry are things that can never be unsaid; sometimes the things that we do are things that can never be undone. Even when anger does not issue in action, when it merely smolders in the breast, it sends its poison through our system; it interferes with our digestive system and with the proper working of mind and body.

Anger is also dangerous for society. There can be little doubt that Jesus had this in mind. The anger against the Romans, fed and kept alive not only by the Zealots but also by the Pharisees, finally boiled over, and precipitated a disastrous war with Rome which ended in the destruction of the Jewish state.

The danger of anger on a large scale is illustrated in our own history. On the first Sunday after Lee's surrender, wrote Washington Gladden in his *Recollections,* the people of the North had in the midst of their joy a sincere pity for the vanquished. He recalled how he, as a young preacher in Morrisania, New York, had said, "I most firmly believe that by a hearty and considerate kindness to the Southern people we can restore the old relations of amity, nay, that we can establish new relations of friendship, which shall be far closer and more enduring than the old ones were."[17]

Any chance that these sentiments might prevail in the nation as a whole, he added, were promptly destroyed in the assassination of President Lincoln. There was a general feeling that the South as a whole was responsible, and popular support swung quickly to the more rigorous, the more vindictive policy of the radical Republicans. The pulpit, which might have been expected to exert a modifying influence, added additional fuel to the flames. Funeral services were held widely over the country on April 19 as Lincoln's body was carried to its final resting place. Most of the preachers, as Gladden recalled, seized the occasion to demand a vigorous policy in dealing with treason. There were exceptions—Henry Ward Beecher, breaking with lifetime associates, and among others, Washington Gladden, an inconspicuous pastor in an unimportant town. "Of the few hundreds who listened," he wrote, "a score may have been convinced, but a voice like this affected the raging of the populace about as much as the chirping of the swallows on a telegraph pole."[18] An emotional cyclone, he continues, swept a whole nation out of the ways of sanity and destroyed the finer growth of tolerance and magnanimity. As a result, seeds of distrust and ill-will were widely and deeply sown, and through the entire period of reconstruction the nation was gathering the harvest.

"For myself," says Gladden, "I must confess that if I had ever cherished any fond belief in the infallibility of the populace, that illusion was forever dispelled by the spectacle of those days. It became only too apparent that a whole people, swept by a flood of excitement, may go hopelessly wrong. Burke says that it is difficult to draw up an indictment against a whole nation. Difficult it may be, but it is sometimes necessary. That entire populations are subject to epidemics of unreason is historically true. And the only hope for this democracy is in the rise of a class of leaders who have the courage to resist the mob, and to speak the truth in the days when the truth is the last thing the people want to hear . . . Our business," he adds, "is to make reason and the will of God prevail."[19]

It is natural and perhaps inevitable that anger should be aroused in our own day by developments at home and abroad. This anger may be turned to constructive ends. We must continually remind ourselves, however, that anger is dangerous. It builds up steam under the boiler, but it takes off the balance wheel. In the years which lie ahead the leaders of our nation and of the United Nations will face tremendous responsibilities. They will make decisions on which the peace and happiness of mankind will depend for generations to come. And these decisions must be governed by reason and sound judgment. If instead they are dictated by passion or determined by hate, our children and our children's children will pay the penalty. More than is ordinarily realized, the emotional attitudes of the American people determine the action of our statesmen. Our duty, as Christians, is to make reason and the will of God prevail.

Jesus said that anger is dangerous. But he goes further: "You have heard that it was said to men of old, 'You shalt not kill; and whoever kills shall be liable to judgment.' But I say to you that every one who is angry with his brother shall be liable to judgment; whoever insults his brother [K.J.V.—shall say to his brother, Raca] shall be liable to [K.J.V.—in danger of] the council, and whoever says, 'You fool!' shall be liable to the hell of fire."

When I was a boy the word "Raca" (in the K.J.V.) never troubled me, for it was not included in my vocabulary. But with the word "fool" it was quite different. I could call my playmates and my brothers according to the flesh every other derogatory word in my vocabulary—blockhead, nitwit, dumbbell, or worse—without concern, but if in the course of events the word "fool" slipped between my lips, I was afraid that I had committed an unpardonable sin and was in dreadful danger of hell fire. Many adults continue to cherish this wooden interpretation of the Bible. But it is not a matter of mere words that Jesus is speaking about. It is the state of heart and mind prompting such expressions that he condemns. A man who is angry at his brother is in danger of the judgment; a man who cherishes scorn or contempt for his neighbor (because he is a Jew, for example, or because his skin is black), a man who outrages his neighbor's personality with even the mildest word of abuse, is in danger of hell fire.

Does Jesus mean that it is always wrong to cherish contempt for one's fellow man or to give outward expression to one's feeling of scorn? I am not sure that he would go so far. It is undoubtedly wrong to cherish contempt for any class or race or nation. I am inclined to think it is wrong also to cherish contempt for any individual, but I am not altogether certain; there are some people whose principles and whose actions really do invite contempt for them as individuals. Jesus does not say that contempt is always sinful or that words of scorn are always wrong. He does make it clear that words of scorn, and the contempt which prompts them, are dangerous. Contempt, his words indicate, is more dangerous than anger. The latter is an emotion which we cannot always control. But the former represents a settled attitude or disposition for which we are fully responsible.

Such contempt is dangerous for the individual. It shrivels up the soul, arouses answering bitterness and contempt in our fellow men, and is liable to bring us under the divine judgment. Therefore if we are in the act of worship and there remember that our brother has some grievance against us, we had better halt our worship and go back and be reconciled to our brother. Jesus suggests that our worship is not acceptable to God until we have repaired the wrong that we have done our brother. We cannot get right with God until we are first right with man. And it is dangerous to delay. If we are not reconciled with our accuser while we are yet free, and while there is yet time, we may find that the prison bars have closed about us, and we will not again be free until we have paid our last penny. It is clear that in this last illustration Jesus is thinking of the nation as well as of the individual. For every patriotic Jew, the one great adversary was the Roman. And as Jesus spoke these words—"Make friends quickly with your accuser," or adversary [K.J.V.]—it was the Roman who would leap at once into his hearers' minds. Change your attitude of mind toward the Roman quickly, Jesus suggested, and seek to come to a mutual understanding, or the nation will inevitably suffer and in the end be drained of its last resources.

Contempt, then, is dangerous, not only for the individual but also for the nation. Philip Lory in *Japan's Military Masters,* written shortly after the outbreak of World War II, tells us that there was a prior time when Japan's military leaders were suffering an eclipse, and when the liberal democratic elements were in the ascendancy. It was shortly after the conclusion of World War I, when democratic tides were sweeping through the world. Then something happened. The Allied leaders at Versailles refused to write into the League of Nations a statement recognizing the principle of racial equality. Opposition came from two sources, the United States and Great Britain. Leaders of these two nations also refused a compromise formula, which required no change in national policy but which would have constituted a face-saving device for the Japanese. This seems strange at first, for the spokesman for the British delegation was Lord Robert Cecil, one of the most uncompromising Christians of his day, and the spokesman for the American delegation was Colonel House, the friend and personal representative of President Woodrow Wilson. These two statesmen opposed every formula proposed by the Japanese because Premier Hughes of Australia threatened, if they were accepted, to stir the current prejudice against Orientals and so to raise a storm of protest not only in the Dominions but also in the western part of the United States. Lord Robert Cecil and Colonel House were afraid to run the risk, afraid that racial prejudice in the United States and Great Britain might destroy the covenant of the League. Mr. Lory describes the consequences in Japan. The liberal democratic elements who desired to make Japan one of the free democratic nations of the world, living in peace and harmony with their fellow nations, were discredited. Japan's military masters resumed control of the nation's policy and began even more rapidly to prepare it for the role it subsequently played in World War II.

Some of us wondered, at the outbreak of this war, at the cold fury of the Japanese against the whites; we were not prepared for the way in which natives of Malaya and Burma seemed to prefer Japanese rule to the beneficient rule of the Anglo-Saxons. But this hatred, this fury, this cruelty of the Japanese, this antipathy of the brown and yellow people for the white, was, in greater measure than most of us realized, an answering response to the contempt which generations of white men had manifested for the colored peoples of the Far East.

"Close observers of the Orient—and some in Africa—," Paul Hutchinson reminded us, "have been warning the West throughout the last twenty years of the rapid rise of racial self-consciousness and pride among tinted peoples. And the whites living in Asia and Africa, it must be admitted, have done little to assuage the racial sensibilities of the native inhabitants. On the contrary many of them have conducted themselves as though it was their purpose to make all yellow, brown, and black men hate the sight of a white. Almost the only exception has been in the case of Christian missionaries.

"In the port cities of China, across the length and breadth of India, in Manila and Singapore and Batavia, and everywhere throughout Central and South Africa, white military and business communities have insisted on social rules of racial segregation which have daily flung the racial challenge full into the faces of the native population. There is some debate as to whether the parks of Shanghai, for instance, ever actually displayed signs reading, 'No dogs or Chinese allowed.' But there can be no dispute as to the fact that Chinese (except nurses in charge of white children) were excluded from the Shanghai parks. Nor that highly educated Chinese, many of them possessing advanced degrees from British and American universities, found themselves excluded from the British and American clubs in that city. The racial bar was maintained with equal rigidity against Filipinos in the American officers' club in Manila. As to the racial laws in South Africa and the white opinion which insists upon them and sees that they are enforced, one can only say that they are probably preparing the way for the most tragic racial conflict the world has ever seen."[20]

In the fall of 1941, Hallett Abend made a tour of the Orient. A native of Java, who was himself friendly toward the cause of the United Nations, gave him this message to carry back to the white men of the West: "Count us up and think it over. We shall be formidable. There are 450,000,000 Chinese; 340,000,000 natives of India; in Thailand and Indo-China there are another 32,000,000 people; Burma and Malaya have 20,000,000. We in the Indies are 70,000,000, the Japanese have 70,000,000, and the Koreans nearly 25,000,000 more. We total more than one billion people, not counting the Arabs, the people of Iran, the Egyptians and others who might side with us, if the white man does not give us real justice. If we are betrayed by the eventual peace, then some Asiatic nation will arise as a genuine and unselfish emancipator, and the ensuing conflict will make the present war [World War II] seem like an amateurish rehearsal."[21]

White Americans cannot afford to be contemptuous of other people. We are faced with the choice of recognizing the colored peoples of the world as our brothers, or of making them an enemy with the advantage of overwhelming numerical superiority. We can never solve our domestic problems, we can never solve our international problems, on the basis of contempt for any people or any race. One of our duties as Christians is to eliminate it from our own hearts and from the heart and thought of the world. It is dangerous to be angry, it is more dangerous to manifest contempt or to cherish it within our hearts. "Make friends quickly with your accuser, while you are going with him to court, lest your accuser hand you over to the judge, and the judge to the guard, and you be put in prison; truly, I say to you, you will never get out till you have paid the last penny."

Adultery and Lust. Matthew 5:27-32

> 27 "You have heard that it was said, 'You shall not commit adultery.' 28 But I say to you that every one who looks at a woman lustfully has already committed adultery with her in his heart. 29 If your right eye causes you to sin, pluck it out and throw it away; it is better that you lose one of your members than that your whole body be thrown into hell. 30 And if your right hand causes you to sin, cut it off and throw it away; it is better that you lose one of your members than that your whole body go into hell.
> 31 "It was also said, 'Whoever divorces his wife, let him give her a certificate of divorce.' 32 But I say to you that every one who divorces his wife, except on the ground of unchastity, makes her an adulteress; and whoever marries a divorced woman commits adultery."

The Old Testament prohibited adultery. But Jesus said that the real sin commenced with the desire and intention cherished in the heart. "Adultery has been committed by any man who allows himself, in the glance of an eye, deliberately to regard a human being as an instrument of lust. The Greek seems to show that our Lord speaks neither of the involuntary occurrence of evil thoughts, nor of the involuntary awakening of the sexual impulse, but of looks whose deliberate purpose is to awaken the latter."[22] It is not everyone who lusts, but everyone who looks to lust, who has sinned in the sight of God.

In verses 28-29, Jesus indicates that "no one should excuse himself on the ground of the weakness of his sensual nature. If his instincts are unruly, he must take heroic measures to subdue them. The eye and the hand are the special instruments of lust."[23] Jesus does not mean that we are literally to cut off our hand or gouge out our eye, but he does mean that we are to cast away the cause of stumbling, whatever it may be, and whatever it may cost.

Matthew inserts here a teaching of Jesus on divorce. The Old Testament allowed divorce, and in Jesus' day this was interpreted by the laxer expositors to mean that a man might put away his wife for any cause. In a day when marriage was the only career open to women this worked great hardship on the woman. Jesus did not attempt to give a divorce law for the state, but according to Matthew's report he did say that in the Kingdom of God divorce was permissible only on the ground of unfaithfulness to the marriage vow. In Mark's Gospel (an earlier account) even this last ground is omitted. (Mark 10:11.) It seems likely, therefore, that the clause, "Except on the ground of unchastity," was added by a copyist and does not represent the original teaching of Jesus. Divorce should never occur among members of the Kingdom; it will not occur if both husband and wife are committed to the ideal of the Kingdom. But what if one spouse or the other is an unbeliever? Paul was forced to deal with this problem in his first letter to the Corinthians. If the unbelieving partner insists on a separation, says Paul, then the believer is no longer bound; there is nothing that he can do. (1 Corinthians 7:15.) Jesus' words, then, are not to be taken as a law to be rigidly enforced by church or state. They do set forth the ideal which Christians should ever strive to realize in practice. In a day when divorce continues to increase ever more rapidly, and when the marriage vow is more lightly assumed, the ideal needs to be emphasized anew.

Untruthfulness. Matthew 5:33-37

> 33 "Again you have heard that it was said to the men of old, 'You shall not swear falsely, but shall perform to the Lord what you have sworn.' 34 But I say to you, Do not swear at all, either by heaven, for it is the throne of God, 35 or by the earth, for it is his footstool, or by Jerusalem, for it is the city of the great King. 36 And do not swear by your head, for you cannot make one hair white or black. 37 Let what you say be simply 'Yes' or 'No'; anything more than this comes from evil."

The Jews had interpreted certain Old Testament passages to mean that only oaths were binding, and not all of them—only the ones in which the name of God was used. Jesus pointed out that all such distinctions are false. All oaths are equally binding. But one should not find it necessary to strengthen his word with an oath. He should recognize that his simple statement is binding, without the use of any stronger affirmation. God is "just as fully implicated by one who says simply 'yes' or 'no' as by any oaths, and whatever exceeds that springs from evil, for it shows that the speaker is not normally conscious of God's interest in his words and acts."[24]

The importance of these words of Jesus should be more apparent in our days when not all commercial advertisements are noted for their veracity, when perjury in the courts has become commonplace, when the word of the politician or the diplomat is no longer trusted.

Revenge. Matthew 5:38-42   Thompson

> 38 "You have heard that it was said, 'An eye for an eye and a tooth for a tooth.' 39 But I say to you, Do not resist one who is evil. But if any one strikes you on the right cheek, turn to him the other also; 40 and if any one would sue you and take your coat, let him have your cloak as well; 41 and if any one forces you to go one mile, go with him two miles. 42 Give to him who begs from you, and do not refuse him who would borrow from you."

The Old Testament permitted "an eye for an eye and a tooth for a tooth." (See Exodus 21:24; Leviticus 24:20; Deuteronomy 19:21.) These verses were generally interpreted to mean that a man could return evil for evil, and in equal measure. Jesus, on the contrary, said, "Do not resist one who is evil," and then gave four examples arranged in descending scale to illustrate what he meant: (1) In case of personal injury—"if any one strikes you on the cheek, turn to him the other also"; (2) in regard to a lawsuit—"if any one would sue you, and take your coat, let him have your cloak as well"; (3) as to official demands, forced service, military or civil—"If anyone forces you to go one mile, go with him two miles"; (4) when it is a request—"give to him who begs from you and do not refuse him who would borrow from you."

How are we to understand these words? Some say that the injunction to "turn the other cheek," for example, should be taken literally—not only by the individual but also by a nation; that followers of Christ should always be pacifists, therefore, even in the most extreme cases. Christians generally are not prepared to accept this interpretation. They point out that Jesus himself did not follow this rule with absolute literalness. When the Jewish authorities ordered him to be smitten, he did not strike back, it is true, but neither did he turn the other cheek; instead he offered a vigorous protest—"If I have spoken wrongly, bear witness to the wrong; but if I have spoken rightly, why do you strike me?" (John 18:23.)

They also point out that if the pacifist insists on taking this one precept literally, he must take the other precepts in the series literally also—refuse to resist evil men, give every man who sues him more than he asks, decline no one who asks him for a gift or a loan. No modern pacifist takes all these injunctions literally. They appear to be inconsistent when they insist that one of the four illustrations shall be so interpreted.

We note again that Jesus' words refer to an injury which is done to oneself. It does not necessarily follow that one is to stand idly by when an injury he can prevent is done to a helpless woman or a helpless child or a helpless nation. Jesus did not command soldiers to abandon their trade.

On the other hand, we ought to consider what these words would have meant to the inhabitants of any land occupied by hostile forces in recent times. To them the words would have meant to abandon any underground movement for deliverance; to bear their conquerors' insults patiently without striking back; when forced labor was required, to do more than was expected. It must have meant the same thing to the first disciples. To Jesus' hearers, "Do not resist one who is evil" would mean primarily, "Do not resist the Romans."

But though the words have immediate application to the particular situation in Palestine there is a principle of abiding value. Jesus means that under no circumstances should we give way to the spirit of revenge and retaliation just described, "an eye for an eye and a tooth for a tooth"; that it would be better to turn the other cheek, to give away our cloak as well as our coat, to go the second mile, for example, than to strike back simply for the sake of revenge. This is the negative principle. More positively, it is Jesus' idea that we should attempt to overcome men's hate by the exercise of active love, a willingness to endure insult, a readiness not only to admit the just claims of our opponents, but to surrender more than absolute justice would require; to do more than we are actually required to do; to give not necessarily whatever any man may ask, but whatever love may suggest.

Jesus' fundamental principle was that evil cannot be destroyed by evil, but only by love. The exact form that love will take depends upon the circumstances. It is a principle that Jesus sets forth and illustrates, rather than an inflexible rule—a principle that has been illustrated again and again in individual experience and world history. Jesus' words offer us the way out of our present predicament just as they offered the way of escape for the Jews of his own day.

Revenge, his words imply, must be repudiated not only by individuals but also by nations.

We won the First World War but lost the peace, and having lost the peace we lost the war as well. One of the reasons why the Versailles peace treaty was not more effective, in the estimation of a great many men competent to express a judgment, was that it was so thoroughly permeated with the spirit of revenge. Messrs. Hoover and Gibson, who lived through those days and sought to discover why the Versailles peace treaty and other such attempts in the past failed to ensure the peace, drew the inescapable conclusion: "Experience shows that no nation can be punished as a whole and, at the same time, leave any hopes for lasting peace."

The London *Economist,* under date of August 12, 1944, arguing against a vengeful peace with Germany, pointed out that the few durable peace settlements in modern times were "those that no large country seriously desired to upset." Those that have been enforced have been mainly between large and small countries. The history of Poland and of Ireland does not "encourage a belief in the possibilities of permanent coercion." In the whole history of western civilization the only wars which have not sowed the seeds of subsequent wars have been those few conflicts which were followed by treaties of peace in which the element of revenge and retaliation was conspicuously lacking.

Yes, it is true as Hoover and Gibson declare: "Experience shows that no nation can be punished as a whole and, at the same time, leave any hopes for lasting peace. This endless treadmill of punishment must be stopped in the world, if there is to be real peace. Victory with vengeance is ultimate defeat in the modern world. We can have peace or we can have revenge, but we cannot have both."[25]

Why is it wrong for a victorious nation to seek revenge on a defeated nation, and why is it impossible for victors to take revenge and find enduring peace? Because such revenge falls inevitably on the innocent as well as upon the guilty, upon children who bore no responsibility for the war whatsoever, upon unborn generations of children who will make up the nation of the future. A vindictive settlement, imposed by the strong upon the weak, arouses answering bitterness and resentment in their hearts and drives them into a new war whenever outside pressure is removed, and as soon as their own resources are sufficient. A magnanimous settlement does not guarantee enduring peace, but it is the only kind of settlement which holds out any such prospect.

If we sincerely desire peace—for ourselves, in our homes, in our neighborhood, within the nation, throughout the world—we do well to heed the words of the Master, to forego all thought of revenge or retaliation, to remember that "Vengeance is mine, I will repay, says the Lord." (Romans 12:19.)

Love. Matthew 5:43-48

Jesus' more positive principle, as we have seen, was that we must seek to overcome evil with good. The principle is formulated more explicitly in the following paragraph:

43 "You have heard that it was said, 'You shall love your neighbor and hate your enemy.' 44 But I say to you, Love your enemies and pray for those who persecute you, 45 so that you may be sons of your Father who is in heaven; for he makes his sun rise on the evil and on the good, and sends rain on

the just and on the unjust. [46] For if you love those who love you, what reward have you? Do not even the tax collectors do the same? [47] And if you salute only your brethren, what more are you doing than others? Do not even the Gentiles do the same? [48] You, therefore, must be perfect, as your heavenly Father is perfect."

Jesus' words apply to one's personal enemies, of course, but also to the enemies of one's nation. The men and women who first heard Jesus would think at once of the Romans, as the inhabitants of any conquered nation would think inevitably of those who had conquered them and who continued to oppress them.

Many men consider these to be visionary ideals that do not take into account the stern world of reality. But Jesus was no visionary, and his words were not spoken in a vacuum, apart from the world situation of his day. His teaching offered a way out, the only way out for the Jews. (Cf. Luke 19:42-43.) And they offer the only way back to health and sanity for our world as well.

What does it mean to love one's enemy? It is important to recall that there are two words in the Greek New Testament, both of which are translated as "love" in the English versions. The first of these words emphasizes the emotional aspect of love, the natural affection of the human heart for the one who is loved; the second word emphasizes the volitional aspect of love, the practical determination of the will to seek the good of the one who is loved. Whenever love is commanded in the Bible as a duty toward one's neighbor or toward one's enemy, it is always this second word that is used and never the first; always the word emphasizing the volitional aspect of love, never the word emphasizing the emotional aspect of love. And it is important to note that this is so. For the average Christian has come to think that "to love" means "to like." As a matter of fact there are some people whom we do not like (at least this is true of most of us). It may be that there are people whom we ought not to like— because of the principles for which they stand, because of their character or lack of character. At any rate we cannot always command our emotions. Therefore many of us have come to the conclusion, consciously or unconsciously, that these words of Jesus hold before us an ideal which cannot possibly be realized in life. But Jesus never says that we must like our neighbors; he never suggests that we must have affection for our enemies. He exhorts us to love our enemies—that is, to desire their welfare, to seek their highest good, whether we like them or not.

Is it possible, or desirable, to love our national enemies? Some do not think so. When our army invaded North Africa in the Second World War, one of our high-ranking American generals said that we must teach our soldiers to hate the Germans with every fiber of their being. Rex Stout, chairman of the War Writers' Board, claimed repeatedly, while the war was in progress, that "the Christian doctrine of love for one's enemies is worse than double talk. It is plain nonsense."

But there were many who disagreed, even at the time. One thing that struck me when I came back from Europe at the end of the First World War was how much more hatred there was among the civilians than there was among men who had been at the front. Most of our leading military men in the Second World War did not find that it was necessary or desirable to arouse artificial hate in our men to make them better soldiers. Ernie Pyle, beloved war correspondent, spoke of Sergeant Buck Eversole as the ideal soldier. "He had no hatred for Germans," wrote Mr. Pyle. "He killed because he had to keep alive himself. 'I'm mighty sick of it all,' he said quietly, 'but there ain't no use to complain. I just figure it this way, that I've been given a job to do, and I've got to do it.' "[26] Americans generally, at home and at the front, seemed to agree with John Steinbeck: "This is a war of finding the target in the cross hairs of the bomb sight and setting the release, and it isn't a war of speeches and frothy hatred. It is a technical job, a surgeon's job; there is only time for hatred among civilians." But there was no time for hatred among civilians either, for they also had their work to do, and hate did not help them to do it more efficiently.

It is very doubtful if hate helped to win the First or the Second World War. It certainly will not help to win a cold war, or to preserve a peace, any peace, for no peace will endure unless it takes into account the legitimate aspirations and needs of all mankind.

George Hudson was born in China, the son of missionary parents. He himself became a missionary to China. He remained in occupied China after most of the missionaries had returned. He was placed in a Japanese detention camp and experienced various indignities perpetrated by his captors. He saw worse brutalities visited upon the Chinese, whom he loved but whom he was powerless to help. His only son enlisted in the Marine corps shortly after Pearl Harbor, and was one of the first of our boys to be killed in the invasion of the Pacific islands. After Dr. Hudson had returned to America he proposed a five-point peace program for the Japanese: (1) Destroy the Japanese military machine; (2) help Japan economically—she must be able to feed her teeming millions; (3) help Japan politically—with a government of her own choosing; (4) help Japan spiritually—this is the task of the church; (5) as soon as possible welcome her back into the family of nations. This, or something like it, was what love required for a people regarded then as our national enemies. And it was not only good religion, but also good, sound common sense. Fortunately it was the policy that was ultimately followed.

In the years that lie ahead we who follow Christ, who desire peace for all mankind, will need to remind ourselves and others again and again of the teaching of our Lord that anger is dangerous, that contempt is dangerous, that revenge must be repudiated, that love, i.e., good will, must be cultivated for all men.

"Love your enemies," says Jesus, "so that you may be sons of your Father who is in heaven." It is only as we do cultivate active good will for those who have only ill will for us, Jesus intimates, that we can live as God's sons, actually enjoy his fellowship, and appropriate his highest blessings. "For if you love those who love you, what reward have you? Do not even the tax collectors [or the Communists] do the same? And if you salute only your brethren, what more are you doing than others? Do not even the Gentiles [or non-Christians] do the same? You, therefore, must be perfect, as your heavenly Father is perfect."

Did Jesus then mean that we could actually achieve moral perfection, that we could actually become perfect even as our heavenly Father is perfect? Certainly he did not, for he makes it clear in one of his parables that when we have done our utmost we must still remember that we are unprofitable servants. (Luke 17:10.) The man whom God will justify is not the man who prays, "God, I thank thee that I am not like other men," but the man who prays, "God, be merciful to me a sinner!" (Luke 18:9-14.) The scientist will never discover complete truth in any field, but he must take that as his goal; the artist will never paint a picture that is ideally beautiful, but that must be his aim; we shall never achieve moral perfection in this life, but that should be our effort.

THE RIGHTEOUSNESS OF THE KINGDOM— ITS OBSERVANCE

Matthew 6:1-18

6 "Beware of practicing your piety before men in order to be seen by them; for then you will have no reward from your Father who is in heaven.

2 "Thus, when you give alms, sound no trumpet before you, as the hypocrites do in the synagogues and in the streets, that they may be praised by men. Truly, I say to you, they have their reward. 3 But when you give alms, do not let your left hand know what your right hand is doing, 4 so that your alms may be in secret; and your Father who sees in secret will reward you.

5 "And when you pray, you must not be like the hypocrites; for they love to stand and pray in the synagogues and at the street corners, that they may be seen by men. Truly, I say to you, they have their reward. 6 But when you pray, go into your room and shut the door and pray to your Father who is in secret; and your Father who sees in secret will reward you.

7 "And in praying do not heap up empty phrases as the Gentiles do; for they think that they will be heard for their

many words. ⁸Do not be like them, for your Father knows
what you need before you ask him. ⁹Pray then like this:

> Our Father who art in heaven,
> Hallowed be thy name.
> ¹⁰Thy kingdom come,
> Thy will be done,
>   On earth as it is in heaven.
> ¹¹Give us this day our daily bread;
> ¹²And forgive us our debts,
>   As we also have forgiven our debtors;
> ¹³And lead us not into temptation,
>   But deliver us from evil.

¹⁴For if you forgive men their trespasses, your heavenly Father
also will forgive you; ¹⁵but if you do not forgive men their
trespasses, neither will your Father forgive your trespasses.

16 "And when you fast, do not look dismal, like the hypocrites, for they disfigure their faces that their fasting may be
seen by men. Truly, I say to you, they have their reward.
¹⁷But when you fast, anoint your head and wash your face,
¹⁸that your fasting may not be seen by men but by your
Father who is in secret; and your Father who sees in secret will
reward you."

1. THE GENERAL PRINCIPLE. Matthew 6:1

The King James Version translates, "Take heed that ye do not
your alms before men, to be seen of them." The Revised Standard
Version has it, "Beware of practicing your piety before men in
order to be seen by them." The American Standard Version translates more literally, "Take heed that ye do not your righteousness
before men, to be seen of them." This is the theme of the section,
for righteousness or piety is a general term which includes alms,
prayer, fasting, all three, and other observances as well.

Jesus has described in the preceding section (5:17-48) the search-
ing character of the righteousness of the Kingdom, its inwardness;
he points out now that its outward expression, its piety or observance, must be sincere, else it has no value in the sight of God.
If we do our righteousness, exercise our piety, perform our religious acts, to be seen of men, then we have our reward but it
comes from men, not from God.

2. SPECIFIC ILLUSTRATIONS. Matthew 6:2-5, 16-18

To make his meaning more clear Jesus applies the principle he has just enunciated to three common religious practices of his own day—alms, prayer, and fasting. He chooses these three because they were at the time the marks of a religious man; also, it may be, because they cover in a way the whole field in so far as the outward expression of a man's religion is concerned. Our religion moves in three directions—inward, outward, and upward; it includes duties toward one's self, toward one's neighbors, and toward God. In the first case it is some form of self-discipline, and in Jesus' day fasting was its best example; in the second case it becomes benevolence, and almsgiving was then its characteristic embodiment; in the last case it is devotion, and prayer was then and is still the typical form. In whatever form our religious life expresses itself, says Jesus, its motivation must be genuinely religious if it is to have any spiritual value.

He takes the giving of alms as his first example. Here is a man who wishes to bestow his charity upon a beggar in the street. He unslings a trumpet, which he carries for such occasions, blows lustily upon it until a crowd has collected, then deposits his coin in the beggar's cap and moves on his way. The illustration is a humorous one and is intended to bring a smile, but it carries the point.

No work of righteousness was more largely inculcated in the Scriptures than almsgiving. (Cf. Leviticus 19:9-10; Deuteronomy 15:7-11; Psalm 41:1; Proverbs 21:13.) And it is a duty which Jesus himself emphasizes (in Matthew 25:31-46, for example). But if we give our alms for the sake of the publicity that it brings, the only reward that we get is the reward of publicity.

"When you give alms," says Jesus, "do not let your left hand know what your right hand is doing." Plainly these words cannot be taken literally; but their meaning, when taken in connection with 5:16, is plain. To have any real value we must give our alms to relieve human need, or to promote God's glory, not merely or chiefly to save our own reputation or to enhance it.

Why do men give today? To escape criticism, to gain the reputation for liberality, to avoid the stigma of stinginess, to keep from paying a heavy income tax, to cover dishonest or unjust means of getting their wealth, to salve their consciences, to help their fellow men, or to advance the Kingdom of God? Motives, no doubt, are generally mixed, but the particular reward that giving brings depends upon the motives that are primary.

Jesus illustrates the principle, in the second place, from the practice of prayer. Quite evidently there were men in his day who wished to gain the reputation for sanctity. They took pains to let men generally know that they prayed. Men are not accustomed today to praying on the street corners, but there are other ways of accomplishing the same end. A speaker at the Harvard Law School once advised the graduates of that school to attend church regularly when they entered upon their practice. "You will meet the best people in the community," he said, "and it will bring you business." He was quite right; a man who goes to church, who observes religious forms and ceremonies in order to make the right human contacts, has his reward, but it comes from men and not from God.

Jesus illustrates his principle in the third place from the practice of fasting. As David Smith points out: "Fasting was not a stated ordinance of the Jewish religion. Public fasts were appointed whenever any public calamity—war, pestilence, drought, famine, and the like—called for humiliation before God; and devout folk fasted privately as they felt the need of spiritual discipline. This, however, was insufficient for the extremer sort of Pharisees. They fasted regularly twice a week."[27] And in some cases, at least, their real motive was to gain the approbation of men. "They make their faces unsightly," our Lord's words might be translated, with a humorous word play which our English version misses, "that they may be a sight to men in their fasting."

Is there any value in fasting (during the Lenten season, for example), or in self-discipline of any sort? Jesus says it all depends on the motive. If you fast because it meets a real need in your soul, well and good; if you do it so that man may honor you or regard you as a pious man, it has no value in God's sight. Your reward in this case comes solely from men.

If we observe any religious practices in order that we may be regarded as religious men, or because of their effect on men, then, says Jesus, we are hypocrites. The word "hypocrite" has come to have a very ugly connotation in our day which it did not necessarily have in Jesus' day. The word comes from two Greek words which meant originally "one under a mask"; in other words, an actor in a play. The hypocrite is one who plays a part. Now there are some men and women who consciously play a part in order to deceive. But there are others who unconsciously play a part; they are often the best actors of all, for they deceive even themselves. Jesus, in his use of this term, refers sometimes to conscious hypocrites; at other times to unconscious hypocrites. Many supposedly religious people who pray and fast and give alms deceive themselves. They really think they are religious. But they are only playing at it. They do not realize that their religion is really a show—to be seen of men; that it has become a form, perhaps even a farce, lacking genuine religious vitality; that it is not prompted by, nor does it promote, genuine fellowship with God.

3. SOME DIRECTIONS ABOUT PRAYER. Matthew 6:6-15

It would seem from a close study of the whole passage and from the parallel passage in Luke, that Matthew, writing topically, as he frequently does, has brought in certain lessons on prayer from other sources. In any case it is eminently proper that here where Jesus has warned against insincerity in prayer other teaching should be assembled which gives us his thought on the way to pray.

As someone has said, "Prayer is a universal instinct, and in every age and under every sky, man has lifted his voice in prayer to God." This does not mean, however, that all men pray regularly; many pray very seldom, if at all, and some profess not to believe in prayer. But when sudden danger comes, or some overwhelming emergency, they, too, are forced to their knees. As the sergeant wrote in the early days of World War II, "There are no atheists in the foxholes of Bataan."

The unfortunate thing is that so many wait until some great need drives them to God and never experience the strength, the insight, and the peace which come from daily communion with the Father as they face the problems, the temptations, the burdens, and the opportunities of life.

Even those who pray regularly know that prayer does not mean to them what it ought to mean and what it might mean if they had mastered the art of prayer. As someone has said, "Prayer is a simple exercise, in which the humblest soul can engage, and yet it is a high art, calling for the best teaching and example, study and effort." We all realize that this is so. How then can we learn to pray? How can we secure more of its values for our own lives? How can we learn to mediate its blessings into the lives of others?

The best way to answer this question is to go to those who have themselves mastered the art of prayer. No one can help us here so much as Jesus. In the passage now before us he tells us something about the method of prayer and then something about the objects of prayer.

The Method—How to Pray. Matthew 6:6-9a

Jesus gave us three valuable hints, all dealing with the fundamentals—what we might call the "A B C" of prayer.

First—*"Go into your room and shut the door and pray to your Father who is in secret; and your Father who sees in secret will reward you."*

What did he mean by this admonition? Did he mean that we were never to pray in public? We know that this was not his meaning, for he himself prayed on the mountaintop and in the Garden of Gethsemane. He prayed when he healed the blind man, when he raised Lazarus from the dead, and when he was hanging on the cross; he went habitually into the synagogue on the Sabbath day, and joined in the prayers of the worshipers. What, then, did he mean when he said, "go into your room, and . . . pray to your Father who is in secret"? He meant, first of all, as the context shows, that we were not to pray to be seen of men. The prayers that we offer in public may be beautiful and eloquent, but if they be not sincerely offered to God they have no spiritual value. We may bow our heads very reverently in Sunday school, prayer meeting, or church, but if we do not join in the prayer, making it our own, it has no value in the sight of God, and no value or beneficial effects for our own spiritual life.

Jesus meant, more positively, that we must try to enter into real communion with God who is our Father. Perhaps this is the first lesson that we need to learn about prayer—the "A" of the "A B C" of prayer. Prayer did not mean to Jesus that God would give him everything for which he asked. When Jesus prayed, he met someone. He came in contact with God.

And so it has always been with the masters of prayer. "Let any of the spiritual seers describe the innermost meaning of prayer to them," says Dr. Fosdick, "and always this habitual attitude of secret communion lies at the heart of the matter; they are seeking God Himself, rather than His outward gifts. As Horace Bushnell says: 'I fell into the habit of talking with God on every occasion. I talk myself asleep at night, and open the morning talking with Him'; and Jeremy Taylor describes his praying as 'making frequent colloquies and short discoursings between God and his own soul'; and Sir Thomas Browne, the famous physician, says: 'I have resolved to pray more and to pray always, to pray in all places where quietness inviteth, in the house, on the highway, and on the street; and to know no street or passage in this city that may not witness that I have not forgotten God.' Ask a monk like Brother Lawrence what praying means to him, and he answers: 'That we should establish ourselves in a sense of God's presence, by continually conversing with Him'; and ask the question of so different a man as Carlyle, and the reply springs from the same idea, 'Prayer is the aspiration of our poor, struggling, heavy-laden soul toward its Eternal Father.' "[28]

And so with us. Prayer is not chiefly asking God for things. It is the loftiest experience within the reach of any soul—communion or fellowship with the infinite God.

To achieve this communion with God, Jesus advises us to go into our room and there pray to our Father who is in secret. It is not necessary, as we have seen, to withdraw on every occasion to our own room, behind closed doors. We must learn to pray, as Jesus did, at all times and on all occasions—to call on God in our time of need, to breathe a hurried petition to him before we begin any new or important undertaking, to ask his blessing in the daily routine of our lives. A friend of mine who has specialized in the study of personal religious living has come to the conclusion that for the average man ejaculatory prayer offered at frequent intervals through the day possesses the richest possibilities. And yet all of us need a place where we can retire from the world and be alone with God. Catholics have found it helpful to use the church for solitary mediation. And some Protestant churches have learned the value of a room especially adapted for communion and mediation. We also need a special time. Most of us prefer to begin the day and to end it with prayer in some favorite spot in our own home, some place where we can shut ourselves off from the world and experience the presence of God.

To pray more effectively, most men have learned to close their eyes and reverently bow their heads or kneel beside their bed. God does not demand some particular posture, any more than he insists on some particular site. We can pray sitting upright in our pews with our eyes wide open, or as we walk down a crowded street. But to close our eyes helps us to forget the world with all of its distractions. To assume a reverent posture helps us to realize that we are in the presence of the Almighty.

Jesus offers another suggestion. *"And . . . do not heap up empty phrases as the Gentiles do; for they think that they will be heard for their many words."* Does Jesus mean that we are not to repeat our petitions, that we are not to pray for the same thing over and over again, that a mother is not to pray day after day and night after night for the safety of her son? We know that he did not mean this, for he tells us repeatedly that we are to be persistent in our prayers. Luke records two parables which illustrate this point. One is the story of a man who had a friend come to visit him late at night, and who found that he had nothing to put before him the next morning. So he went to a neighbor's house and knocked and called out for bread. But the neighbor replied that he and his children had gone to bed, and that it was too late to get up and give him any food. The man kept on knocking and calling out for bread until finally his neighbor rose and gave it to him, not because he was his neighbor but because he wanted some sleep that night. And Jesus said we were to pray with the same persistence with which that man knocked and called for bread. (Luke 11:5-8.) Then he told the story of a woman who went to an unjust judge and asked him to settle a case for her. The judge refused to listen, but the woman hounded him continually, day after day, until finally he settled the case, not because he wanted justice to be done but because he wanted some peace in life. And Jesus said we were to pray with the same persistence with which that woman pressed the unjust judge day after day for justice. (Luke 18:1-8.) We must not misunderstand the meaning of these parables. Jesus did not mean that we must beg God for his gifts; he did mean that we must have the same persistence in our search for the spiritual goods of life that we do in our search for the material things of life. There are some things that God is not able to give us until by persistent prayer we have prepared our hearts to receive them.

We come back to the main proposition. Jesus said, "Use not vain repetitions." (k.j.v.) If he did not mean that we were not to ask for the same thing over and over again, what did he mean? He meant exactly what he said, that we were not to use *vain* repetitions. Or as Dr. Goodspeed renders the verse in his American Translation, "Do not repeat empty phrases." Or as Moffatt puts it, "Do not pray by idle rote like pagans, for they suppose they will be heard the more they say." Heathen think that prayer acts like magic. Some Roman Catholics think that there is value in counting their beads so many times and in repeating so many Ave Marias. Protestants, too, sometimes use meaningless words and repeat meaningless phrases. Grace before meat is a beautiful custom and should be continued, but it tends to become an empty form. The phrase "for Christ's sake" is added at the end of our prayers, and often without meaning to God or to ourselves. We repeat habitual phrases and customary petitions like a parrot, perhaps the usual prayer before retiring, or it may be even the prayer which our mother taught us to pray, and we think we are really praying. But as Friar Lawrence phrases it, we are only "fooling ourselves with trivial devotions."

In this connection Jesus reminds us that God knows what we have need of before we ask. Some people wonder, Why, then, should we pray? But anyone who thinks that we pray to inform God of our needs has not learned the first lesson in prayer. God knows that we have need of food, but he expects us to work to obtain it, for such effort is essential for man's highest development. God knows that we have need of knowledge, but he expects us to study to secure it, for mental exertion is likewise necessary. He knows that we have need of spiritual good which we cannot obtain by the labor of our hands or by the effort of our minds, but he expects us to pray that we may receive it, for fellowship with God and conscious dependence upon him are necessary for our highest development along spiritual lines. We do not pray to inform God or to persuade him, but to fill a very necessary condition for prayer's answer. "We are not moving God toward us, we are raising ourselves to him." Or as Augustine said long ago: "Prayer cleans and purifies the heart and makes it more capable of receiving the divine gifts. God is always ready to give us his light, but we are not always ready to receive it. By prayer we open channels through which blessings are always ready to flow." "And in praying use not vain repetitions." This is Jesus' second suggestion, the "B" of the " A B C" of prayer.

"Pray then like this: Our Father who art in heaven." Here Jesus gives us a third fundamental lesson on how to pray. We are to pray to God who is our Father, who loves each one of us

as though there were only one of us to love, who is more ready to give good gifts to his children than any earthly father is to give gifts unto his children.

We are to pray to God who is our Father *in heaven*—whose views are not bound as ours necessarily are by the things of earth or by the things of today, a God who sees what is best for us in all the years that lie ahead, through all the years of eternity—a God who has all power at his disposal, who makes the wrath of men to praise him, and who makes all things work together for good to them that love him.

We are to pray to *our* Father who is in heaven, not my Father only, or your Father, but our Father, the God and Father of all men everywhere. A certain United States Senator once announced that the boundaries of the United States were the boundaries of the brotherhood of man. Nazis taught that the brotherhood of man was bounded by the blood and soil of Germany. The Japanese were taught to believe that they were the descendants of the sun goddess, they and no one else. Jesus taught that God is the Father of all men, and that ideally all men are brothers. And when we pray, we are to pray to God who is not merely my Father or your Father, but the God and Father of all men everywhere.

As Walter Rauschenbusch pointed out, the model prayer which follows is not one that can be offered selfishly. Every petition is a petition not only for ourselves but also for others. And the spirit of the Lord's Prayer is to be the spirit of all our prayers. Perhaps our prayers have been ineffective because we have prayed for ourselves and for those whom we love, but not for all men everywhere; because we have unconsciously assumed that God is the Father of white men but not of black men, of Americans, but not of Europeans or Asiatics. When I was a boy I used to pray sometimes that God would let me win a game in which I was engaged. In other words, I was hoping that God would give me something that he would not give my opponent. I was assuming that God was willing to play favorites. Some of us never outgrow this childish conception of prayer. We have forgotten, or perhaps we never really understood, the full significance of Jesus' saying, "Pray then like this: Our Father who art in heaven."

The Objects—What to Pray For. Matthew 6:9b-15

When the disciples asked Jesus to teach them how to pray (Luke 11:1) he taught them that familiar prayer which we call the Lord's Prayer. He repeated it also (or Matthew has seen fit to include it) in the Sermon on the Mount, telling them to pray "like this." He does not mean that we should pray only for those objects mentioned in his model prayer. He himself went easily and naturally to the Father with everything that was on his heart, and so should we. Yet there is much that we can learn about the legitimate objects of prayer from a careful study of the six petitions in the Lord's Prayer.

We note, to begin with, that three of the six petitions—and these the first three—refer to the things of God. We gather from this that we should pray for God's interest as well as our own. Perhaps that is the trouble with our prayers—we have prayed for our own needs and the needs of our family, but have forgotten to pray for the wider needs of the Kingdom. We gather, in the second place, that we should put the interests of God first, our own interests second. This does not mean that we must always mention the divine interests first, though perhaps it would help to put us in the proper mood and to put our personal petition in the proper frame of reference if we did so more often. But even when the petitions which we voice are altogether for our own needs, the wider interests of God should be in mind. Even in the midst of life's tragedies we should pray as Jesus did in the Garden of Gethsemane, "Nevertheless not my will, but thine, be done." (Luke 22:42.) It may be that our prayers have not meant to us what we should like because, selfishly, we have sought our own interests to the neglect of God's interests, or because, subtly, unconsciously, we have sought our own interests at the expense of the divine interests. But what are the divine interests?

"Hallowed be thy name"

The name of God in the Bible represents the character of God, God as he has revealed himself to man. To hallow means to make known as holy on the part of God and to regard as holy on the part of man. When we pray, "Hallowed by thy name," we pray that God will reveal to us the holiness of his character, of his purpose, and of his will—as we pore over his revealed Word, as we delve into the secrets of nature, as we seek to understand the meaning of world events, as we try to interpret the meaning of our own experience.

As we offer this petition we pray that we and other men may recognize and reverence the character and purpose and will of God as revealed to us in the Bible, in nature, in history, and in our own experience. And if our petition is vital and sincere, we pledge ourselves to reverence and to lead other men to reverence God's character, God's purpose, and God's will, however it may be revealed to us.

"Thy kingdom come"

The Kingdom is God's rule over individual men and over society, in this world as well as in the world to come. When we offer this petition we pray that God's reign may be established in our hearts, in our homes, in our city, and in the social, industrial, political, and international life of our times, and we pledge ourselves to work toward the accomplishment of that end. We also pray for that glorious consummation of the Kingdom when Jesus shall come again in the glory of the angels.

"Thy will be done"

When we offer this petition we pray that God's will may be done by whom? Certainly not by God, for such a prayer would be both futile and foolish. We request, then, that God's will may be done by other men, by our neighbors, by heads of governments, by local politicians, by industrialists and labor leaders, by all men in every walk of life, by British, and Chinese, and Russians. But such prayer is meaningless unless it is also and first and foremost a prayer that God's will may be done in us.

"Thy will be done on earth."
On bended knee we pray;
Then leave our prayer before the throne,
And rise and go our way.

And earth is filled with woe,
And war, and evil, still,
For lack of men whose prayer is, 'Lo,
I come to do Thy will.'

Thy will be done on earth?
Lord, grant me grace to see
That if Thy will is to be done,
It must be done by me.[29]

This petition is not only a pledge that we will seek to do God's will but also that we will accept God's will for our own lives when it runs contrary to our own wills; that like Jesus we are able to say, "Nevertheless not my will, but thine, be done." (Luke 22:42.) It means also that we are ready to bring all our desires, all our petitions, all our aims and ambitions, to this test, and that they will be left subject to this condition. In the early days of World War II, an English minister told this story: "A good Christian man said to me that he hoped our airplanes would fly over German cities and kill as many of their children as their airplanes had killed in our cities. I told him that if he really wished this he ought to put it into a prayer. He thought for a moment and answered, 'No, of course you couldn't ask God to do that and end up "for Jesus Christ's sake." ' " Perhaps a good many of our wartime prayers and a good many of our present-day desires and plans might be ruled out by this test.

The reverencing of God's character, the coming of God's Kingdom, the doing of God's will—these are the great ends toward which our prayers should be directed. But we have other needs, needs of a more personal character, that it is proper for us to present unto God. So Jesus taught us to pray, "Give us this day our daily bread."

"Give us this day our daily bread"

We gather from this petition that it is proper for us to ask God for the material blessings of life. "Daily bread" probably means the bread that is necessary for the day, or the bread for today that will be needed tomorrow. Jesus does not encourage us to ask for superfluities. The petition covers what is needed for culture and refinement, but it does not cover luxury and extravagance. Moreover, it is a social prayer. Jesus teaches us to pray not only for ourselves, but also for our fellow men—Give *us* this day *our* daily bread. No man who sincerely prays this prayer can take advantage of his fellow men or refuse to minister to their need.

Shortly after the end of World War II, a woman wrote the following letter to *Time*:

> "I am an American housewife. I have lost a son in this war, and I am not going to tighten the belts of my other children to feed Europe. I find my friends, clubwomen, etc., feel the same way. I, like thousands of others, donated in the 1920's to feed starving Europe. I was a traitor to my son. Now I say, let them stand on their own feet and work out the problem they have brought upon themselves."

This woman wrote out of the bitterness of her soul; but so long as that mood persisted, she could not pray sincerely the prayer which our Lord taught us to pray—"Give us this day our daily bread."

If we offer this petition with understanding and with sincerity, then we pray that all men in all nations, and every group and class within our own nation, may have food and clothing and shelter which they need for their physical well-being, and we pledge ourselves to labor for an economic order in which this may come to pass.

"Forgive us our debts"

Jesus taught us in the previous petition to pray for our material needs (not our material wants). He comes now to our spiritual needs. The first petition looks to the past and the second to the future. As we think of the past we realize that we have sinned and we pray that God may forgive us our failures, our shortcomings, and our sins; that he may forgive the sins of our nation and the sins of the blundering, suffering race of men.

We pray that God may forgive us as we have forgiven those who have wronged us. The "as" must not be pressed to mean that the fullness of the Father's forgiveness is to be measured by the extent to which we forgive our fellow men. No such hard bargaining is to be understood. What is meant is that we ourselves must cultivate the spirit of forgiveness toward those who seem to have wronged us before we venture to claim forgiveness for ourselves, or before we can really appropriate the forgiveness of God. This is the one petition in the entire prayer on which Jesus comments: "For if you forgive men their trespasses, your heavenly Father also will forgive you. But if you do not forgive men their trespasses, neither will your Father forgive your trespasses."

To forgive our debtors does not mean that we must necessarily forget the injury that has been done us. It may be impossible for us to forget, and at times even unwise. Yet very often that would be the very best thing we could do. Many of us allow the memory of some fancied wrong or of some real injury to rankle in our memories and to send its poison through our systems, when the best thing we could do for our mental, spiritual, and sometimes even for our physical health would be to forget the injury, to put it resolutely out of our minds forever.

To forgive our debtors does not mean that we must always act toward the offender as though the offense had never been committed. That might be an unwise procedure for both parties concerned. Yet often that is what should be done. If some of us would determine that from this time on we were going to act as though some word which hurt us had never been spoken, or as if some deed which injured us had never been performed, we would be surprised at the sense of release it brought us, and at the new fellowship with God it made possible.

To forgive may mean to forget, to act as if some word had never been spoken, or some deed had never been done; it certainly means that we shall not seek revenge, that we shall not only welcome but actually seek a reconciliation (which may of course be thwarted by the offender himself), and that we shall continue under all circumstances to be motivated by good will toward the offender.

The disciples who first offered this prayer would necessarily think of their national enemies as well as those who had injured them personally. To them it must necessarily have meant, Forgive us our debts as a people as we forgive the Romans. And so today. We pray that God will forgive us as we have forgiven not only our personal enemies but also our national enemies.

It is curious that Christians repeat this petition so often while their hearts are filled with bitterness toward those who have injured them (often it is only an imaginary slight). It is strange how Christians continue to mouth these words while they seek vengeance against their national enemies and the punishment of generations that are still unborn.

Adolf Keller tells how representatives of the church finally met in Geneva, some years after the First World War, to prepare for the first great World Conference of Churches. "The French delegates refused to enter into negotiations before the Germans confessed their sole guilt for the war and repented. The conference was on the point of breaking off. Then the Moderator of the Waldensian Church, Signor Giampiccoli, stood up and said: 'Dear brethren, I lost two sons in the war and yet I feel nothing in my heart towards the brethren from the belligerent countries other than peace and love. What we need are not human declarations, but the grace of God for the overcoming of our sins. Let us pray the Lord's Prayer together.' "[30] So they prayed, and it was this petition, "Forgive us our debts, as we also have forgiven our debtors," which saved in its infancy the great ecumenical movement which has now grown to such proportions, and which holds such promise for the future. One of the greatest contributions that Christians can make now toward world peace is to pray sincerely and to teach others to pray—"Forgive us our debts, as we also have forgiven our debtors."

"And lead us not into temptation"

This petition looks to the future, as the preceding one looks to the past. As we look back we recognize our failures, our mistakes, and our sins, and we ask God for his forgiveness. As we look toward the future, we think first of our weakness, and we pray, "Lead us not into temptation." The form of this petition is somewhat puzzling, or would be if it were not so familiar. Does God lead us into temptation? We recall the words of James: "Let no one say when he is tempted, 'I am tempted by God'; for God cannot be tempted with evil, and he himself tempts no one; but each person is tempted when he is lured and enticed by his own desire." (James 1:13-14.) Dr. C. C. Torrey reminds us that Jesus spoke in Aramaic, and that our oldest manuscripts of the New Testament give us only a Greek translation of the words which he actually spoke. If the Greek words are translated back into the Aramaic, and these in turn are translated into English, Dr. Torrey claims that the phrase would read, "And let us not yield to temptation." This, or something like it, must be the real meaning of Jesus' words.

There is another point to be noted. The word translated "temptation" refers to trials as well as to temptations to sin in the sense in which we commonly use the term. Jesus does not encourage us to pray that we may escape trial and suffering in life, or that we may escape temptation. Both are inevitable, bound up with our finite existence here on earth. We are urged to pray only that our trials may not be too great for our strength and that our temptations may not be such that we cannot overcome them. We pray not only for ourselves but also for our children and for the children of other parents and for the children of other lands, that they may not be subjected to temptations which are greater than they can overcome or to trials which are greater than they can endure.

As we offer this petition we acknowledge our own weakness, but also the strength of God which is available to us. We pray that in him we and those whom we love, and not only they but all men, may find strength to overcome selfishness and sin, anxiety and depression and fear and bitterness and resentment, that we and they may live triumphant and radiant lives and in the midst of all life's trials know the peace of God which passeth understanding. And as we offer this petition, we pledge ourselves to work for a world in which our children and the children of other men may not be tried or tempted above that which they are able to endure; we pledge ourselves to continuous and unceasing effort to make known to all men the divine resources which are available to them.

> "For thine is the kingdom, and the power, and the
> glory, forever. Amen"

These words, which follow in the King James Version, were not a part of the original prayer and are not contained in the Revised Standard Version. But they were added, we feel, through a very sound instinct on the part of the early church. They give us the reason it is proper for us to offer the prayer. "For thine is the kingdom, and the power, and the glory, forever. Amen."

In looking back over this prayer we note that Jesus puts the emphasis first on the interests of God, next on man's spiritual needs, and last on man's material needs. Some of us reverse Jesus' order. We pray most earnestly for material blessings, less earnestly for spiritual blessings, least earnestly for the things of God.

If we wish to learn the secret of successful prayer, we need to consider over and over again these very simple and yet profound words of Jesus: "When you pray, go into your room and shut the door and pray to your Father who is in secret . . . And in praying do not heap up empty phrases as the Gentiles do . . .

Pray . . . like this: Our Father who art in heaven, Hallowed be thy name. Thy kingdom come, Thy will be done, On earth as it is in heaven. Give us this day our daily bread; And forgive us our debts, As we also have forgiven our debtors; And lead us not into temptation, But deliver us from evil. For thine is the kingdom and the power and the glory, forever. Amen."

THE RIGHTEOUSNESS OF THE KINGDOM—ITS VALUE

Matthew 6:19-34

The second and major section of the Sermon on the Mount deals as we have seen with the righteousness of the Kingdom. In 5:17-48 Jesus describes its nature; in 6:1-18 its observance; in this third subsection, 6:19-34, its value, or the place that righteousness, which is the mark of the Kingdom, must hold in our lives. We must put it absolutely first, says Jesus, above all worldly ambitions (19-24) and above all worldly anxieties (25-34). The key verse is 6:33—"Seek first his kingdom and his righteousness, and all these things shall be yours as well."

Some think that the first division (19-24) applies primarily to the rich, and the second (25-34) primarily to the poor. The well-to-do, they say, are tempted to lay up treasures upon earth; it is the poor who are anxious about the necessities of life. But this is not a valid distinction. All of us worry, whether we are rich or whether we are poor, and we are all tempted to lay up treasures on earth. As a matter of fact, Jesus was speaking to a group of Galilean peasants, none of whom could be accounted rich. "It is the poor," Theodore H. Robinson points out, "whom He is exhorting not to store up treasures for themselves on earth, as is shown from the language He uses. 'Break in' is literally 'dig through,' and recalls the mud and wattle hut of the poorest countryman, through which a thief with a knife or trowel would work his way in half an hour on a dark night. Yet even such a hut may contain a scanty hoard of coin, grain, or some fabric which moth and rust may corrode."[31] Money can be just as great a peril to the poor man as to the rich man, and will be, if he makes it the goal of his life. As for worry or anxiety, that is certainly not the prerogative of any class.

Jesus' words, then, apply equally to rich and to poor. We are all exhorted to seek first God's Kingdom and God's righteousness.

1. ABOVE WORLDLY TREASURES. Matthew 6:19-24

> 19 "Do not lay up for yourselves treasures on earth, where moth and rust consume and where thieves break in and steal, 20 but lay up for yourselves treasures in heaven, where neither moth nor rust consumes and where thieves do not break in and steal. 21 For where your treasure is, there will your heart be also.
>
> 22 "The eye is the lamp of the body. So, if your eye is sound, your whole body will be full of light; 23 but if your eye is not sound, your whole body will be full of darkness. If then the light in you is darkness, how great is the darkness!
>
> 24 "No one can serve two masters; for either he will hate the one and love the other, or he will be devoted to the one and despise the other. You cannot serve God and mammon."

What does Jesus mean when he says, "Do not lay up for yourselves treasures on earth"? He does not mean that we are to make no provision for our old age or for our children, nor even that we are to avoid all accumulation of wealth. "This He never condemned," says David Smith. "On the contrary, He represented it as a sacred trust and commended the good and faithful servant who diligently improved it (cf. Matthew 25:14-30). And His own earthly experience shows how precious an opportunity it affords; for did He not owe His daily bread to the kindness of prosperous disciples who 'ministered unto him of their substance' (cf. Luke 8:3)? It is a Christian duty to be 'diligent in business' that not only may we 'owe no man anything' but be able to succor others in their need." [32]

When Jesus tells us not to lay up treasures on earth, he forbids us to set our hearts on them, to accumulate them for their own sake, to make them the end of life, to use them selfishly, forgetting our obligations to others. "What he condemns is not riches, but trust in riches; not money, but the love of money." Our real treasure must be not on earth, but in heaven.

But how can we lay up treasures in heaven? Jesus gives us no indication here, but there are other verses which make it clear, i. e., Luke 12:33-34: "Sell your possessions, and give alms; provide yourselves with purses that do not grow old, with a treasure in the heavens that does not fail, where no thief approaches, and no moth destroys. For where your treasure is, there will your heart be also"; Matthew 19:21: "If you would be perfect, go, sell what you possess and give to the poor, and you will have treasure in heaven; and come, follow me." The injunctions to "sell what you possess" were given to particular individuals for a particular purpose, and were not given to Jesus' disciples in general. Nevertheless, it is made clear that we lay up treasures in heaven by using our worldly resources for the good of our fellow men. That is made still clearer in Luke 16:9: "And I tell you, make friends for yourselves by means of unrighteous mammon [i.e., money], so that when it fails they may receive you into the eternal habitations." Paul is more specific still: "As for the rich in this world, charge them not to be haughty, nor to set their hopes on uncertain riches but on God who richly furnishes us with everything to enjoy. They are to do good, to be rich in good deeds, liberal and generous, thus laying up for themselves a good foundation for the future, so that they may take hold of the life which is life indeed." (1 Timothy 6:17-19.)

Paul's words make it evident that we lay up treasures in heaven not only when we bestow alms, but also when we do good; not only when we give money, but also when we give our services. Some have money to give; others have talents, professional skill, business ability, or scholarly aptitudes. It is not the size of the gift that counts, but the spirit. That Jesus made quite clear as he commented on the widow's mite: "This poor widow has put in more than all those who are contributing to the treasury. For they all contributed out of their abundance; but she out of her poverty has put in everything she had, her whole living." (Mark 12:43-44.)

Why should we lay up treasures in heaven instead of treasures on earth? Jesus gives us four reasons:

First, earthly treasure is transient. Some of it perishes (moth, rust); or it passes out of our hands (thieves, or it may be the stock market); in the end we leave it all behind. Heavenly treasures on the other hand are permanent; we enjoy them in this life and through all eternity. This is the first reason. Our earthly treasures are transient; it is foolish, then, to accumulate wealth here and to make no provision for the years of eternity.

Second, earthly treasure steals our heart, for "where your treasure is, there will your heart be also." In Jewish psychology the heart was not only the seat of the emotions, but also that of the intellect and the will. One's treasure engrosses his affections, commands his thoughts, and determines his purpose. If a man lives for money, or for wealth, it affects his whole inner life. "His aim is to add to it, his anxiety is that it might disappear; all his hopes and fears, ambitions and doubts, are concentrated on it. This means that the thing steals the man's very soul, and he is no longer able to concentrate on that which should absorb him— God and His Kingdom. Instead of lifting his heart to heaven, he has buried it with his savings."[33] As Maclaren comments: "Where your treasure is, there will your whole self one day be."

Third, earthly treasure blinds our vision. Jesus uses here a physical fact to illustrate a moral trait. First, the physical fact. The eye is the lamp of the body. If it is sound (Goodspeed), if it focuses properly, then our whole body is full of light, i.e., we have clear and accurate vision. If it is unsound, diseased, blinded, or improperly focused, if it sees doubly (two objects where there should be one), then we walk more or less uncertainly; we are walking in the darkness, darkness which of course may be more or less complete. What Jesus means to say is this: If we recognize that God's Kingdom and his righteousness are the highest moral values in life, then we have clear moral vision, we can distinguish between good and evil, we are walking in the light. On the other hand, if our real treasure is on earth, then feeling, emotions, intellect, will, are all affected; our moral vision is impaired, our moral judgments are distorted, conscience is no longer a safe guide, we are walking in the darkness. This truth is abundantly illustrated in life. If a man puts money first, there is no crime on earth which he will not commit. The lower type of criminal commits arson, robbery, murder. The higher type of criminal resorts to fraud, chicanery, and deceit. Unscrupulous businessmen make false claims in their advertisements, adulterate their goods, cheat their own government—even in time of war, when men's lives are at stake. None of us is altogether exempt. It is an unfortunate fact that no one of us can see clearly where his own economic interests are involved. Long ago the prophet Amos pointed out that there are rich and powerful men who "do not know how to do right." (3:10.) Even good men and good women rationalize their conduct and justify the practices of the group or class to which they belong. They can drive daily past the miserable dwellings and living conditions of the poor, they can pass through a great depression which deprives ten million men of the means of livelihood in their own country and helps to plunge the world into chaos, and never even question the economic policy which promotes their own immediate prosperity and dooms others to hopeless poverty. Not even the sound of thunder on the horizon, the voices of multitudes of men demanding better conditions of life, overthrowing traditional forms of government, and surrendering cherished and hard-won liberties, arouse them from their moral and spiritual complacency. One of the most disturbing things that comes to a student of church history is the way in which again and again the moral judgments of the church—its leaders and its people—have been warped by the economic interests of the individuals who compose the church.

According to Jesus we judge clearly, as individuals and as a group, only when we seek first God's Kingdom and his righteousness.

Fourth, it is impossible to serve God and mammon. Pitirim A. Sorokin in *The Crisis of Our Age* finds here the tragedy of our modern civilization: "Investing all his energies in the control of nature, sensate man achieved a conspicuous degree of success. But in this process he lost his *self-control*. Becoming—like a child toying with a bomb—infatuated with the physical forces at his disposal, in an access of madness he directed them against himself and his own achievements. In his eagerness to serve mammon he forgot to serve God, and he now pays the tragic price of his folly!"[34]

In Jesus' day, mammon was a morally neutral term and meant wealth or riches or money. Jesus says we must put either God or mammon first. One must be subordinate to the other because they make opposing claims on our lives. Here is a way by which we can make more money, but it is not a way which God can approve. What are we going to do about it? Here is a cause which needs financial assistance. God would like for us to help, but we have other uses for our money—what are we going to do about it? No man can serve God and money, for both claim the whole man. We must choose, therefore, which we will serve, which we are going to put first.

But though we cannot serve God and money, we can serve God with money. One of the best ways in which a man with business talents can serve God is to make money, to make it honestly and fairly, paying wages which are equitable, to make it in a business that helps humanity, and then to use his money for the good of mankind and for the glory of God.

2. ABOVE WORLDLY ANXIETIES. Matthew 6:25-34

25 "Therefore I tell you, do not be anxious about your life, what you shall eat or what you shall drink, nor about your body, what you shall put on. Is not life more than food, and the body more than clothing? 26 Look at the birds of the air: they neither sow nor reap nor gather into barns, and yet your heavenly Father feeds them. Are you not of more value than they? 27 And which of you by being anxious can add one cubit to his span of life? 28 And why are you anxious about clothing? Consider the lilies of the field, how they grow; they neither toil nor spin; 29 yet I tell you, even Solomon in all his glory was not arrayed like one of these. 30 But if God so clothes the grass of the field, which today is alive and tomorrow is thrown into the oven, will he not much more clothe you, O men of little faith? 31 Therefore do not be anxious, saying, 'What shall we eat?' or 'What shall we drink?' or 'What shall we

wear?' ³²For the Gentiles seek all these things; and your heavenly Father knows that you need them all. ³³But seek first his kingdom and his righteousness, and all these things shall be yours as well.

34 "Therefore do not be anxious about tomorrow, for to-morrow will be anxious for itself. Let the day's own trouble be sufficient for the day."

Jesus tells us that we are to seek first God's Kingdom and his righteousness, putting it above all worldly ambition and also above all worldly anxiety. In the King James Version we read, "Take no thought for your life, what ye shall eat, or what ye shall drink." This injunction is repeated in verse 31, "Take no thought, saying, What shall we eat? or, What shall we drink?", and again in verse 34, "Take therefore no thought for the morrow: for the morrow shall take thought for the things of itself."

This is an unfortunate translation, one that is not true to the original Greek and which holds up an impossible ideal for our present day. If there is any father or mother who does not take thought for the material needs of his family he is derelict in his duty. If there is any boy or girl, any businessman or labor leader, any soldier or statesman, who does not take thought for the morrow, he is inexcusably stupid. When we read this passage and a number of others like it in the Bible, we need to remember that language sometimes changes its meaning. The word "manufacture," for example, originally meant to make by hand, but now it means to make by machinery. The word "spinster" originally referred to a woman who spun. Now it describes an entirely different type of individual. There was a time when it was a compliment to refer to a woman as homely (meaning home-loving); now one uses the adjective at his own peril. The King James Version, which many Christians continue to read, was translated from the original Greek in 1611, back in the days of William Shakespeare. Shakespeare uses the expression "take no thought" in the sense of "take no anxious thought," and that was the meaning which the phrase had to the men who translated the King James Version. The Revised Standard Version brings out the meaning better for our present day—"Do not be anxious about your life"; "Do not be anxious about tomorrow." Weymouth in the third edition of one of our modern translations, trying to bring out the exact shade of thought, translates, "Do not be over-anxious." Moffatt translates, "Never be troubled." Goodspeed in his American translation comes still closer to our American idiom—"Do not worry about your life, wondering what you will have to eat or drink, or about your body, wondering what you will have to wear. . . . Do not worry about tomorrow, for tomorrow will have worries of its own."

Jesus does not say, "Take no thought." There never was a time, perhaps, when men needed to take more careful thought about so many things. What he does say is, Don't be troubled, don't be anxious, don't worry about the material necessities of life, or about the future—what it will bring to you or to your loved ones.

He proceeds to give us three reasons why we should not so worry.

Worry Is Generally Unnecessary. Matthew 6:25-26, 28-30

God gave us life. It stands to reason that he will sustain us with the food and the clothing that we absolutely need. "Look at the wild birds; they sow not, they reap not, they gather nothing in granaries, and yet your heavenly Father feeds them. . . . Look how the lilies of the field grow; they neither toil nor spin, and yet, I tell you, even Solomon in all his grandeur was never robed like one of them." (Moffatt.) If God feeds the birds he will feed us; if he clothes the lily, he will also clothe us.

Superficially it might seem that Jesus teaches that food and clothing will come without effort on our part. But this is to misunderstand the figure. As a matter of fact, few men have to work as hard for their living as birds do. They spend most of their time looking for something to eat. But they don't seem to worry about it. They appear carefree and happy, and every now and then they pause and pour out their heart in song.

You do not have to worry about your livelihood, says Jesus. God, who provides an opportunity for the birds to secure their food, will also provide an opportunity for you. In seeking to understand the meaning of these words for our own times, we need to remember that they were spoken to men who lived in Palestine almost two thousand years ago. Palestine was a poor country, and many were hungry for bread. Yet it was a simple agricultural civilization; no one was far from the land, and few, if any, actually starved. In the first century A.D. in Palestine, Jesus' words may have been literally true. Undue concern about the necessities of life was unnecessary. God who provided sufficient supplies for the birds had also provided sufficient supplies for them.

Is this still true in our own day? Some think so and are convinced that no man who trusts in God sufficiently, who seeks first his Kingdom and his righteousness, will ever come to want. We will have to admit that this trust, this assurance of God's fatherly care, does sometimes produce a very beautiful sort of piety, and that sometimes it does seem to produce some very remarkable results. Nonetheless, this interpretation does not agree with the total experience of life. And sometimes it encourages a disparagement of our fellow men which is unwarranted, or justifies action or inaction on our part that is altogether inexcusable. It suggests that men who meet poverty and want are lacking in piety or in consecration and therefore do not need our sympathy and help. As a matter of fact, conditions today are very different from what they were in Jesus' day. We do not live in an agricultural civilization but in an urban civilization, an industrial civilization. If anything happened to shut off the food supply of any one of our great cities, thousands would go hungry in a very brief period, no matter how much they trusted in God. During the great depression of 1929, when millions of men were out of work through no fault of their own, there were many fathers and mothers who trusted in God, but who nevertheless saw their children hungry for lack of food. In recent years, myriads of men and women and children in Asia and Africa and Latin America have suffered want and many of them, we can be sure, have had greater faith in God than multitudes who suffered not at all.

God has provided resources by which the needs of all of his children may be supplied, but through ignorance, indifference, or sin, we have deprived many men of the necessities of life. Jesus foresaw that this would be the case. In his parable of the last judgment he said, "I was hungry and you gave me no food, I was thirsty and you gave me no drink . . . As you did it not to one of the least of these, you did it not to me." (Matthew 25:42, 45.)

Jesus' words do not mean, then, that the man who is dedicated to the ideals of the Kingdom will always be free from want. Yet such is generally the case. We may not have the frills of life. We may not have all the luxuries that we want. But most of us do have, and will continue to have, the necessities of life. A doctor who had many patients with incomes in the higher brackets made a careful study of the things that they worried about. He found that forty per cent of these things never happened; thirty per cent were about things that were entirely beyond their control; twelve per cent were about physical ills that were caused or greatly aggravated by their own emotional attitudes; ten per cent were about friends or members of their family who were perfectly able to look after themselves; leaving eight per cent which really needed some attention. And even here their worry did not help. An analysis of our own worries would probably yield similar results. Most of our worries are unnecessary. We are like the man who said, "I have had more troubles than anybody in the world, and most of them never happened."

Worry Is Always Unavailing. Matthew 6:27

I once knew a boy whose greatest ambition was to be tall. He wanted to be at least six feet and, if possible, to have a few inches to spare. When he failed to grow as he thought he should, he began to worry about it, and he continued to worry for many years. But all of his worry did not add one inch to his stature—which is the point that Jesus makes. "And which of you by being anxious can add one cubit to his stature?" (R.S.V. margin.) Once I had thick black hair. When it began to fall out and then to turn gray, I worried a great deal. But all of my worry did not stop the inexorable course of nature. It does not help a young girl to worry about the lack of attention she receives from her boy friend; it does not help a businessman to worry about the problems of his business; it does not help a mother to worry about the safety of her son. To take the proper sort of thought is valuable, of course, but worry is the enemy of clear thought. It dissipates our energies and leaves us less capable of solving the problems that we face. As someone has said: "Worry fritters away wealth and ushers in poverty; it is the dismisser of friends and the herald of enemies; it drives peace from homes and instills corroding strife; it clouds the intellect and fosters failure." The young girl who worries about the lack of attention of boy friends is likely to find, as a result, that she is less attractive to them; the businessman who worries about his business will find that he is less able to think clearly about the problems that confront him; the mother who worries about the safety of her son may find, if she is not very careful, that she is only adding new burdens to those which her loved ones already carry.

The preferred R.S.V. translation of 6:27 reads: "Which of you by being anxious can add one cubit to his span of life." Goodspeed again puts it more nearly in the American idiom: "Which of you with all his worry can add a single hour to his life?" The meaning is the same, whichever rendering we choose. We can undoubtedly add to the span of our lives by taking thought—about our diet, for example; or about our regimen of work, rest, exercise, and play; or about the way in which we drive on the highways. But worry does not add any years to our lives; not even "a single hour."

Rather the opposite. Dr. Flanders Dunbar once made a careful study of men and women who had passed the century mark. Her survey revealed that long life is due to no one secret but to a blend of ingredients. Seven of eleven factors isolated were closely related to the elimination of worry. The study suggests what we otherwise know to be a fact, that worry is not only unavailing, but also positively harmful.

Kirkpatrick and Huetner in an authoritative book, *The Fun-*

damentals of Health, say: "The worst enemy of efficiency as well as the best ally of nervousness is worry." At a meeting of the American Psychiatric Association, Dr. Dunbar asserted that worry puts many persons in the hospital, even gives them angina pectoris pains, and sometimes hastens death. "Emotional factors," she added, "may play a role in the development of chronic invalidism or hasten fatal termination of heart disease. Detection and relief of conflict and anxiety is one of the major problems of convalescence and of the utmost importance in preventing relapses and invalidism." Eminent doctors have asserted that fifty per cent of our ills are due to emotional attitudes, of which anxiety or worry is one of the chief.

Most of our worries are unnecessary; all of our worries are unavailing, and on the other hand are positively harmful. But there is a third reason that Jesus gives.

Worry in a Christian Is Unbecoming. Matthew 6:31-32

When I was a boy I read a book (by Robert Louis Stevenson, I think) which told about a boat caught in a storm in one of the southern seas. It was off a rock-bound coast and there was danger every minute that the boat would be blown against the rocks and dashed to pieces. The passengers were ordered to remain in the cabin, and there they were, all huddled together, fearful that every moment would be their last. Finally one of the passengers, more daring than the rest, left the cabin and made his way along the deck until he came to where he could see the pilot, lashed to his post, and slowly inch by inch turning the boat out to sea. The pilot turned, saw the lonely watcher, and smiled. Immediately the encouraged passenger made his way back to the cabin, and burst in on the startled group of watchers with the glad tidings, "All's well. I have seen the pilot's face, and he smiled." So it is with us. No matter how dark the night, how rough the storm, or how many rocks there are ahead—if only we have seen our Pilot's face, we know that all is well.

In the Gospels we read about another storm, which broke upon the Sea of Galilee. The disciples, hardened fishermen though they were, were terrified. They went to Jesus, who was asleep in the stern, awoke him and said, "Teacher, do you not care if we perish?" Jesus, we are told, rebuked the wind, and immediately there was a great calm. Then he turned to the disciples and said, "Why are you afraid? Have you no faith?" (Mark 4:38-40.) Did Jesus mean that because he was with them in the boat they should have known that no harm could befall them? It could not have been that, for Jesus never promised his disciples physical security. He told them, on the other hand, that they must be prepared to suffer. When Mark's Gospel was written, in Rome, the disciples there had just undergone a very severe persecution. Many had been cruelly tortured. Some had been covered with pitch and set on fire to furnish light for Nero's garden party. Others had been clothed in the skins of wild animals and mangled by wild dogs. Those who survived knew that Jesus did not mean his presence would save them from physical disaster. What, then, did he have in mind? What would the early church have us understand by this familiar story? There is only one thing he could have meant or that the early church could have understood that he meant. We are to trust God, not only in the calms, but also in the storms of life. Why should we be afraid of death? In life or in death, this is still our Father's world. We do not know what the future will bring to us or to those whom we love. We only know we cannot drift beyond his love and care.

It is natural for a pagan to worry, says Jesus; but for a Christian to worry betrays a subtle lack of confidence in God. It indicates that in this respect, at least, we are but little better than the pagans.

We will all agree that these are three excellent reasons why we should not worry. Most of our worries are unnecessary, all of them are unavailing, and for a Christian to worry is unbecoming. We all know this, but what we need is something to keep us from worrying. Does Jesus give us any practical help along this line?

Undoubtedly he does. But before we consider what he has to say, let us recognize very frankly that this problem of worry is more difficult for some than it is for others. We have different temperaments and different constitutions. I am blessed, or it may be burdened, with a rather even disposition. I am naturally phlegmatic, I seldom get excited, and hardly ever wax enthusiastic. My imaginative powers are rather weak. I do not project myself easily into the lives of other people. I tend naturally to live in the present, not in the past or in the future. Other people, including some of those whom I know best, are built quite differently. I am glad this is true, for otherwise life would become very dull indeed. They are highstrung, imaginative, keyed up, and tense. They become highly enthusiastic about many things, and because of this, through the action of certain natural laws, they tend at times to become depressed. They project themselves into the lives of other people; they rejoice with those who rejoice, and suffer mentally and sometimes physically with those who suffer. Such people tend naturally to worry more than those of a more phlegmatic disposition. Excessive worry is due sometimes also to one's physical condition, to the state of one's nerves, to the secretion or to the lack of secretion of some gland. Then, too, worry tends to become a habit, and like all habits, it is one that is very easy to form and very difficult to break. If one is accustomed to carrying his worries with him to bed, it is natural that he should wake up about three o'clock in the morning and find it very difficult to go back to sleep. In addition there are some who have more difficult problems to face and heavier burdens to bear than others.

But though some will be able to overcome this habit of worry much easier than others, all of us can make progress toward that desirable end if we will determine to follow the practical suggestions that Jesus offers.

"Do not be anxious about tomorrow, for tomorrow will be anxious for itself. Let the day's own trouble be sufficient for the day."

As we have seen, the rendering of this verse in the King James Version of the Bible is very misleading. Jesus does not say, "Take no thought for the morrow," but, "Do not be anxious about tomorrow." In the American translation—by Goodspeed—it reads:

"Do not worry about tomorrow, for tomorrow will have worries of its own. Let each day be content with its own ills."

Do not worry until you have to. Do not borrow trouble before it comes. Do not worry about tomorrow's trouble, Jesus says, with a touch of humor, for each day has troubles enough of its own. If each day has its own troubles, it is certainly unwise to worry about troubles that may not happen and probably will not happen. It is better to worry about today's troubles and let tomorrow take care of itself. Take one day's troubles at a time.

Someone has suggested that we have here a concession to human nature. Jesus had told us not to worry, but he knows men and women and recognizes that all of us will worry more or less. So he says at the last, if you do worry just worry about today's troubles; do not worry about tomorrow's troubles until tomorrow. This is excellent advice.

"You have a disagreeable duty to do at twelve o'clock. Do not blacken nine and ten and all between with the color of twelve," says George Macdonald. "Do the work of each and reap your reward in peace. So when the dreaded moment in the future becomes the present, you shall meet it walking in the light, and that light shall overcome its darkness. No man ever sank under the burden of the day. It is when tomorrow's burden is added to the burden of today that the weight is more than a man can bear. Never load yourself so. If you find yourself loaded, at least remember this: it is your doing, not God's. He begs you to leave the future to him and mind the present. In all our difficulties, perplexities, trials, it will help us to remember that we have to take but one step at a time. Let us ask God to help us to take that one step bravely and unfalteringly. Tomorrow's strength is very largely the heritage of today's patient striving."

I will never forget how that lesson came home to me. When I was a boy I was beset with anxieties. I worried about many things, but if everything else gave out for the moment, there was always one thing which I could and did fall back on—and that was my next visit to the dentist's chair. I had very bad teeth; every six months I went to the dentist, and there were always six or more cavities to fill. The grinding instrument which dentists use made a great deal more noise when I was a boy than it does now, and it struck a nerve much more frequently, or so it seems to me at the present time. And every time I got up out of the dentist's chair, I began to worry about my next visit, six months hence. One day it came home to me that after all this was a very foolish way to live, so I decided to enjoy myself for five months and crowd all of my worrying into the last thirty days. It worked so well that when the last month came I decided that I would not worry for three more weeks but would do all of my worrying during the last seven days. When that week came, I decided that I would go for six more days before I began to worry; and when the day came, I decided I would wait until I got into the dentist's chair; and when I got into the dentist's chair, I decided I would wait until the drill struck the nerve, and then I would pack all of my worrying into those few swift seconds of concentrated pain.

I do not claim that I have consistently followed the insight that came to me at that time. But I have tried from that day to this not to worry about anything until it actually happens. Increasingly I have learned to follow this procedure. And I find it saves a tremendous amount of wear and tear on my nervous system. I have made few discoveries that add so much to my happiness and peace of mind. For ninety-nine times out of a hundred the thing I am tempted to worry about does not happen, and when it does, somehow I always find grace from God to meet it.

And so it will be with you. You may find it difficult at first, but if you persist you will find that it becomes easier with time and with practice. You, too, will find that it conserves nervous and physical energy, that it adds tremendously to your peace of mind. For most of the things you are tempted to worry about never happen. And if they do—those little things, which after all are so unimportant, or those great things on which your life's happiness seems to depend—you, too, will find grace from God to meet them. God said to Paul, "My grace is sufficient for you." (2 Corinthians 12:9.) And God's grace is sufficient for us. It is always sufficient for the needs of the day. It becomes insufficient, I am sometimes inclined to think, only when we add imaginary ills to real ones, when we join future troubles with present ones, when we forget that each day's trouble is sufficient for that day.

Jesus does not forbid us to take thought for the morrow; he does advise us not to worry about tomorrow until tomorrow comes. One way to overcome worry is, in this respect at least, to live one day at a time.

"In everything by prayer and supplication . . . let your requests be made known to God." (Philippians 4:6.)

Jesus suggests prayer as one of the remedies for anxiety in Matthew 6:33 and again in Matthew 7:7-11. The hint is made more explicit in Paul's letter to the Philippians: "Have no anxiety about anything, but in everything by prayer and supplication . . . let your requests be made known to God. And the peace of God, which passes all understanding, will keep your hearts and your minds in Christ Jesus."

This is one of the most comforting promises in the Bible. But there are many Christians who feel, consciously or unconsciously, that it can never be realized in real life. It sounds to them like those words which we speak to our friends in their times of need, words which it is so easy for us to speak to others, but so difficult for us to apply to ourselves. I am sure the Philippian Christians did not feel that way. I can see them, in my mind's eye, in Lydia's parlor as these words are read to them for the first time. I can see them turning every man to his neighbor and saying, Do you not remember how Paul and Silas prayed and sang hymns of praise when they were here in our Philippian jail, with their bruised and bloody backs, and with their feet far apart in the stocks? (Acts 16:19-25.) Those Philippian Christians knew what we would do well to remember, that Paul was not writing words that were magically dictated to him from heaven, but that he was writing to them out of his own deepest experience. He was passing on to them the secret of his own life, a secret which he had proved in a life of hardship and trial.

"Have no anxiety about anything." How can we help being anxious, with so many things pressing in upon us at the present, and with so many uncertainties for the future? Paul tells us. "Have no anxiety about anything"—that means the little things of life and also the big things; *"but in everything"*—that includes the big things, but also the little things—*"by prayer and supplication . . . let your requests be made known to God. And the peace of God, which passes all understanding, will keep your hearts and your minds in Christ Jesus."*

Many times I had gone to God in my own times of trial, and I had not always found that peace of which Paul is speaking. Perhaps that has been your experience, too. Then one day, it was a good many years ago now, I discovered a little phrase in this great verse that I had never noticed before (it has been omitted heretofore in the quotation of this verse; I wonder how many of you who read these words have noticed the omission), that little phrase *"with thanksgiving."* I have come to believe, not from anything that I have ever read in any book, for I never read it there, but simply from my own experience and from the experience of others with whom I have talked, that this little phrase is the key to this great promise. I have never gone to God in prayer in my own time of trial—in times of mental strain, or in times of physical danger, as in the First World War—with thanksgiving, thanksgiving for the blessings which I have enjoyed in the past, thanksgiving for the blessings which I enjoy in my hour of deepest distress, thanksgiving for the grace of God which is always available to me through Jesus Christ—I have never gone to God by prayer and supplication, with thanksgiving, without finding something at least of that peace of which Paul is writing.

Prayer is the greatest source of emotional stability. That is a well-recognized psychological fact. But if prayer is to be most helpful it needs to follow the pattern prescribed by Paul, "In everything by prayer and supplication with thanksgiving let your requests be made known to God."

"Seek first his kingdom and his righteousness."

Jesus tells a curious story about a man who was tormented by a demon. (Luke 11:24-26.) One day the demon was induced to leave, and the man was mentally at peace. But no healthier interest came to take the place which the demon had occupied, and ultimately the demon returned with seven other demons, and they all drove their pitchforks into the man's body and mind so that his last condition was infinitely worse than his first. It is not enough to banish one devil, or seven devils, Jesus says, unless we put something positive and constructive in its place.

Is it possible to exorcise permanently the demons of worry and anxiety and fear? Is there anything so great and compelling that there is no room left for these devils in our lives? Jesus says that there is. There is one thing that banishes worry and destroys the very reason for its being. "Do not be anxious, saying, 'What shall we eat?' or, 'What shall we drink?' or, 'What shall we wear?' . . . But seek first his kingdom and his righteousness, and all these things shall be yours as well." We will continue to worry just so long as we are supremely concerned about our own lives, our own interests, our own plan for our lives. We will cease to worry when we become supremely concerned about God's reign in the hearts of men and God's rule over the lives of men, when we have learned to pray as Jesus prayed in the Garden of Gethsemane, "Nevertheless, not as I will, but as thou wilt."

J. Wilbur Chapman said: "One of my friends told me that he stood one morning on one of the highest peaks of the Rocky Mountains, bathed in the sunlight of a perfect day. He looked down from where he stood and saw a tremendous storm raging in the valley. As he looked, suddenly up from the dark clouds came a black body. He looked again and still a third time and the great black object became a Rocky Mountain eagle, measuring seven feet from tip to tip of its wings. As I looked, he said, the eagle mounted higher and higher, clear above the clouds, and fighting his way through the storm soared high above my head, every feather wet with the raindrops, and every raindrop sparkling like a jewel in the sunlight, and I stood and watched him until he was lost in the face of the sun."

So it is with us. We are living in the valley, and we cannot always dissolve its clouds, but we can rise above them into the sunlight of the presence of God.

Jesus says, "Seek first his kingdom and his righteousness, *and all these things* [food, clothing—the necessities of life] *shall be yours as well.*" This promise is generally true even when applied to the individual. As a matter of fact, however, it was spoken to a group. (In the Greek, which distinguishes between "you" singular and plural, this is very apparent.) As Conrad Noel puts it: "The promise that all material necessities will be abundantly provided to those who seek God's Kingdom and his justice was not, in fact, given to individuals as such, but to individuals in a company which was already becoming the nucleus of the new world. If they were to establish the divine commonwealth on the foundation of God's justice, if a world of men were to spring up in which greed had given place to generosity and domination to service, in which men co-operated to produce, instead of competing to destroy,"[35] then there would be enough for all, none of them would lack the necessities of life.

In the book of Acts we read how that promise began to be fulfilled: "And all who believed were together and had all things in common; and they sold their possessions and goods, and distributed them to all, as any had need." (Acts 2:44-45.) There came a time when this simple practice of Christian brotherhood would not suffice; the church then developed those brotherly services which played such an important part in its victory over the Roman Empire and which laid the foundation for the charitable agencies and institutions of our present day.

Economists tell us that now we have passed from an economy of scarcity to an economy of abundance. In simplest terms, this means that for the first time in human history we are actually able to grow more food and produce more goods than people require for the basic necessities of life.

The United Nations Conference on Food and Agriculture, meeting in Hot Springs, Virginia, May 1943, stated: "This conference, meeting in the midst of the greatest war ever waged and in full confidence of victory, has considered the world problems of food and agriculture and declares its belief that the goal of freedom from want of food, suitable and adequate for the health and strength of all peoples, can be achieved. . . . There has never been enough food for the health of all people. This is justified neither by ignorance nor by the harshness of nature. Production of food must be greatly expanded; we now have knowledge of the means by which this can be done." But there is this important qualification, "It requires imagination and firm will on the part of each government and people to make use of that knowledge." We might add that it requires not only imagination and firm will but also good will.

And here is the rub. Because we do not have proper imagination, or a will which is sufficiently firm, or enough of genuine good will, we have the strange anomaly of business cycles—prosperity and depressions, people starving in the midst of plenty, machines idle with materials on hand and men out of work—because people do not have the money to buy what the machines can produce.

When an economy of scarcity prevails, poverty, ignorance, disease, and war are inevitable. But they are not inevitable, at least in the same degree, in an economy of abundance.

This means that the role of the church and the message of religion must change. It is the same gospel but it has a different emphasis. In an economy of scarcity (when there was not enough food and not enough goods to satisfy men's needs) it was natural and perhaps inevitable that churchmen should stress resignation on the part of the poor and charity on the part of the rich. It is not surprising that many pictured life as a dreary pilgrimage and promised men "pie in the sky by and by."

There will always be need for resignation and perhaps for charity. The church will always need to remind men that life is a pilgrimage, and that we must look forward to a city whose maker and builder is God. But in an economy of abundance, there should be a different emphasis. Not charity but justice. Not resignation but a crusade to obtain security and economic opportunity for ourselves and others.

This determination that all men shall have economic security and opportunity to share in the good things of life is not only good religion but enlightened selfishness, or, as we might say, plain common sense.

World War II proved what machine production can do when production is co-ordinated and guided toward a single goal; when artificial limitations imposed by the desire and the necessity for profit have been removed. As a writer in *Harper's Magazine* (December 1944) pointed out: "In the prewar year 1940 the value of the goods and services produced in the United States had reached the record figure of 97 billion dollars. By the end of 1943 we had practically doubled this record. We were producing at the estimated rate of between 188 and 190 billion dollars. Certainly that doubling of national production in less than four years was one of the most remarkable events in all economic history."

People of other lands know what machines—plus government regulations and priorities—can do when they produce for consumption rather than for profit. If they cannot find security and opportunity to share in the good things machines can produce under the traditional economic system they will wreck it and rear something else in its stead.

George Counts uttered a word of warning: "We have learned from the experience of a tragic quarter-century that if men are forced to choose between liberty and bread, they will take bread, or perhaps even the promise of bread. America's championship of the common man, which has been genuine, must now vindicate itself vis-a-vis the quickly grown Russian giant which has relegated economic crises and unemployment and applied with unexampled rigor to the many and diverse races and peoples living within the borders of the Soviet Union the Christian and democratic principle of equality. If we have in this country a recurrence of severe depression with the fear, pain, and bitterness that it engenders, the appeal of Russian Communism will grow like wildfire." [36]

The Cleveland Conference, attended by representatives of all the churches, spoke to the same point: "Over a century and a half ago it was given to the American people to determine by struggle and experiment whether government by the people could be established and maintained on the earth. Upon the success of this adventure rested a great hope for mankind. In the intervening years the growth of the United States as a home for human freedom has been a notable fact and influence. It must now be demonstrated that human freedom is compatible with economic security. [The experience of the last quarter of a century reveals that great masses of people will sacrifice the former for the promise of the latter.] A new challenge is offered [therefore] to the people of America to establish along with political democracy an opportunity through productive employment to earn an income sufficient for the basic needs of food, clothing, shelter, health, recreation, and cultural pursuits, and assurance to every individual of whatever race of an equal and unsegregated opportunity for worship, protection in time of unemployment, illness or need, and full political and civil rights." [37]

Here is the question. Can we build a society based not on selfish gain primarily, and not on compulsion, but on the Christian motive of service and love to mankind? The first two ways are broad and easy ways, but they lead to destruction. The last is a straight and narrow way, but it leads to life, for individuals and for society.

Jesus points the way in the Sermon on the Mount—"Seek first his kingdom and his righteousness, and all these things shall be yours as well." (Matthew 6:33.) If Christian men will seek above all other things to extend God's reign and to establish righteousness and justice in the earth, no one will go hungry or suffer for lack of the necessities of life. To bring about such a state is a primary Christian responsibility. We are to seek first God's Kingdom and his righteousness in hope and expectation that the time will come when "all these things" shall be ours as well.

THE RIGHTEOUSNESS OF THE KINGDOM— ITS GAINING

Matthew 7:1-12

7 "Judge not, that you be not judged. ²For with the judgment you pronounce you will be judged, and the measure you give will be the measure you get. ³Why do you see the speck that is in your brother's eye, but do not notice the log that is in your own eye? ⁴Or how can you say to your brother, 'Let me take the speck out of your eye,' when there is the log in your own eye? ⁵You hypocrite, first take the log out of your own eye, and then you will see clearly to take the speck out of your brother's eye.

6 "Do not give dogs what is holy; and do not throw your pearls before swine, lest they trample them underfoot and turn to attack you.

7 "Ask, and it will be given you; seek, and you will find; knock, and it will be opened to you. ⁸For every one who asks receives, and he who seeks finds, and to him who knocks it will be opened. ⁹Or what man of you, if his son asks him for a loaf, will give him a stone? ¹⁰Or if he asks for a fish, will give him a serpent? ¹¹If you then, who are evil, know how to give good gifts to your children, how much more will your Father who is in heaven give good things to those who ask him? ¹²So whatever you wish that men would do to you, do so to them; for this is the law and the prophets."

No earnest Christian can follow the Sermon on the Mount to this point without being conscious of his failure to attain the high ideals of the Kingdom. How can we measure up to such standards? How can we realize such lofty ideals in our own life? Jesus seems to deal with these very practical questions in 7:1-12. He gives us three simple but far-reaching rules by which we may grow in the right direction, three rules for living which we might term the keys to the Kingdom. Religion, as we have seen, moves in three directions—inward, outward, and upward. It inculcates duties toward self, duties toward our neighbors, and duties toward God. In the first case it is self-discipline; in the second case it is benevolence; in the third case it is piety. These three rules for living apply to these three realms. We are to judge *ourselves* before we judge our neighbors; we are to do unto *others* what we would have them do unto us; we are to ask *God,* knowing that he is more ready to give good gifts to us than any earthly father is to give good gifts to his children.

1. "JUDGE NOT, THAT YOU BE NOT JUDGED." Matthew 7:1-6.

What did Jesus mean by this injunction? Did he mean that we are never to pass any judgment on the moral worth of our fellow men, on their character or on their actions? We are certain that he cannot have meant that, for we are bound to form judgments, and a nature that does not react against evil is itself immoral. In the great struggle between good and evil, a man cannot remain morally neutral. To attempt to do so would be to pass judgment upon himself.

In addition we have Jesus' own example. He describes Herod very aptly as "that fox"; he characterizes the scribes and Pharisees as hypocrites; and in 7:6 he urges his followers to exercise discernment. We are to take man's character into account. Not to do so involves danger for ourselves and for others. We must, for example, use tact and discrimination in our presentation of Christian truth. We are not to put the holiest things of our religion before men who we know will befoul them—*"lest they trample them underfoot and turn to attack you."*

If this be the case, what does Jesus mean when he says, "Judge not, that you be not judged"?

He means for one thing that we are not to be censorious in our judgments. We are not to be "critical" of our neighbors. We are not to go around looking for the bad while at the same time we overlook the good. We are not to magnify the evil out of all proportion to the good.

Jesus means also that we are to be careful in forming our judgments and especially in transmitting them to our neighbors. We should not transmit them if they are derogatory judgments unless we are certain of our facts, and unless it is necessary or helpful for us to do so. Perhaps he meant, also, that they should be tentative judgments, subject to revision in the light of subsequent information or in the light of changed conditions. It is a good rule to accept as final no adverse judgment passed by men on their fellow men until we have had an opportunity to verify that judgment by direct observation, or in some actual experience, or by some other incontrovertible evidence; and even then not to hold the judgment as absolute. It is so easy for all of us to misjudge men, to form our judgments on mistaken facts or without full knowledge of all the facts.

Froude tells that once when he and Carlyle were out walking, a blind beggar came and asked assistance. Carlyle gave him a sixpence and then waited to see what he would do. The dog led the blind man straight to the nearest public house. "I suppose," says Froude, "I made some contemptuous remark, but Carlyle only said, 'Poor devil, if we knew how he came to be what he is, perhaps we would not be so hard on him.' " If we only knew how the men we meet have come to be what they are, perhaps we would not be so hard on them.

How little we know of the burdens men bear or of the temptations they face! A single word, a single act (that can be so easily misjudged), even repeated words, or acts that have become frequent, do not tell the whole story. And as long as life continues there is always the possibility of change, the chance of amendment.

We must be cautious in our judgment of groups as well as of individuals. Surely Jesus must have had this in mind. His words, spoken originally to Jews, would mean, "Do not judge the Romans, for with what judgment you judge, you yourselves shall be judged, as individuals and as a nation." All of us have the tendency to form mental pictures of groups other than our own, and these mental pictures are likely to be caricatures and unfair therefore to the individuals who compose the group and with whom we come in contact. The picture we form of the Jew, the Negro, the Russian, the Japanese, certainly does not fit all Jews, or all Negroes, or all Russians, or all Japanese. To form a judgment of any group, or class, or race, or nation, based on isolated details, or partial facts, or inadequate or distorted data, is not only absurd but also dangerous and sinful.

We need to be particularly careful in the judgment that we form of individuals and groups that we do not like. For here especially we are likely to put the worst possible construction on the facts and to be the least careful in checking to see if the facts are really true. We need to be most careful, perhaps, in forming judgments regarding individuals or groups whom we do not like, and whom our neighbors, or the members of our social class, do not like. For here the tendency to err is multiplied manyfold by the attitude of our friends and neighbors. Every student of public affairs knows that the mass mind becomes unreflective and is moved more by its prejudices than it is by rational deliberation. The mass mind is created not only by demagogues whose artifices are apparent to the instructed, but also by newspaper, radio, television, and currents of national feeling.

In times of industrial strife there is grave danger that we shall judge the mass of laboring men, who desire above all else an opportunity to improve their standards of living and to gain economic security, by the action of a few labor leaders whom we do not like, or by the practice of some of the more unscrupulous unions. Others of us, in similar fashion, tend to judge industrialists by the record of a few industrialists who are labor baiters and exploiters of their fellow men. In the heat of World War II many Americans were led to believe that all Japanese were inherently brutal. Only gradually did we learn that stories of atrocities could be balanced by stories of unexpected kindness.

We have not yet come to the heart of this passage, to the main point that Jesus had in mind, but let us pause for a moment to note that this sin of judging our neighbors rather than ourselves, of passing quick, superficial, careless judgment on individuals and groups, is a very common sin, and one that has its dangers for our moral and spiritual life and also for our social health and for the peace of the world. It is a sin from which very few of us are free, a besetting sin of Christians as it is one of the besetting sins of all men. One reason for this may be that it exalts our own ego. Most of us suffer from a feeling of inferiority, a sense of inadequacy. To realize that the best of men have feet of clay, to recognize that our neighbors have faults or weaknesses which we ourselves do not possess, gives us a certain sense of superiority. We enjoy gossiping about the frailties of our fellow men because it blinds us to our own frailties and our own inadequacies. My neighbor is as weak as I am, in this respect he is weaker than I, and so I glow with a sense of moral superiority. The cheapest way to exalt one's self is to debase someone else. If only we would look into our own hearts and be perfectly honest with ourselves, I think we would admit that there are times, at least, when this diagnosis is correct.

But there is another reason. We are prone to believe the worst about some group or class other than our own, in some cases at least, because it helps to excuse our action or to justify our lack of action. At the height of the world depression (1929) when ten million men were out of work in our own land, some people actually persuaded themselves that these men were to blame for their own misfortune and that all of them could find work if they really wanted it. It was certainly a comfortable belief, for it deprived them of all sense of responsibility. There was no reason why they should make any sacrifices or countenance any change in the *status quo* which ministered to their own welfare and presumably rewarded all men according to their just deserts.

This sin of judging our neighbors rather than ourselves is not only a very common sin, but also a very subtle one, and one of the most difficult in the whole catalogue to recognize. We discern it very easily in our neighbors, but not in ourselves. I well remember, in one of my summer pastorates while a seminary student, how an old couple "entertained" me during the whole period of my visit by criticizing their neighbors near and far. Nothing I could say or do succeeded for very long in diverting them from this delectable pastime. At the close of the evening they said, with all sincerity, "The worst thing about this community is that the people here are so critical of their neighbors; thank God, that is one thing no one can say about us."

Jesus gives us two reasons why we should avoid this critical attitude, this proneness to judge others rather than ourselves.

First, it is dangerous and leads to our own judgment: *"Judge not, that you may not be judged yourselves; for as you judge so you will be judged, and the measure you deal out to others will be dealt out to yourselves."* (Moffatt.) From whence does this judgment upon ourselves come? Jesus does not say. Perhaps he means that if we adopt a critical attitude toward others they will adopt a critical attitude toward us (which is certainly true), or he may mean, as David Smith thinks, that thus unwittingly we have judged ourselves. It may very well mean, and probably does mean, that this habit of judging others rather than ourselves is a sin which will bring us into the divine judgment.

Second, it is inconsistent, or as Jesus says, hypocritical. To quote Moffatt's translation: *"Why note the splinter in your brother's eye, and fail to see the plank in your own eye? How can you say to your brother, 'Let me take out the splinter from your eye,' when there lies the plank in your own eye? You hypocrite! take the plank out of your own eye first, and then you will see properly how to take the splinter out of your brother's eye."* We need to recall here again that "hypocrite" in the biblical sense means an actor. It may refer to one who consciously plays a part; it refers more frequently, perhaps, to one who unconsciously plays a part, and probably does so here. There are some, no doubt, who consciously condemn their fellow men in order to conceal their own more serious failures. But the number is comparatively rare today and was in Jesus' day as well. To be always judging our neighbor rather than ourselves is hypocritical, Jesus suggests, because we have faults of our own, and commonly our faults are greater than those we notice in our neighbors—to use Jesus' humorous illustration, we see the splinter in our neighbor's eye, but overlook the plank in our own.

It is not true, of course, that we always have more serious faults than do those whom we criticize. But always there are faults, and some very serious ones, and it may be that if we had been tempted or tried as they have been tempted and tried, we would have failed even more seriously than they.

John Bradford, a celebrated English clergyman, is reputed to have remarked, as he saw a poor wretch being led to the gallows, "There but for the grace of God goes John Bradford." The saying is also attributed to Richard Baxter, the eminent Puritan leader of the seventeenth century, and to John Newton, who wrote some of our most beloved hymns, and to a number of other distinguished servants of the church. Any one of the group might have said it, for the most eminent saint will be the first to realize that he might have fallen as other men have if he had faced the conditions that some other men have faced.

Not to recognize this fact, Jesus says, is hypocrisy—not conscious hypocrisy, perhaps, but certainly unconscious hypocrisy (i.e., play-acting). In other words, we are living in a make-believe world and not facing facts. In addition it is often our critical attitude toward our brother that prevents us from seeing our own faults. The man who is always criticizing the faults of his neighbor is generally blind to his own. We point out the fault in our neighbors' lives and that gives us a feeling of self-righteousness which makes us blind to our own defects. All of us who criticize need to echo the words of Burns:

> "O wad some power the giftie gie us
> To see oursels as ithers see us!
> It wad frae monie a blunder free us,
> An' foolish notion."

This is true not only of individuals, but also of groups. An editorial in *The New Republic,* written shortly before the end of World War II, said, "There is a theory that the war was caused solely by the personal devil embodied in Germans and Japanese. The devil was there; he can appear in almost any human being and almost any nation, given the appropriate circumstances. We must not forget in what circumstances he waxes great. It was not an accident that the great depression, originating in America in 1929, hit Germany harder than any other nation, and that Hitler rose to power in the year after unemployment reached its peak."[38] Not to recognize that the same germs which produced such a terrible disease in Germany are also latent in our own society and, given the appropriate circumstances, might become virulent is to live in a fool's paradise.

And this brings us to the positive part of Jesus' injunction and to the main point that he had in mind: *"First take the log out of your own eye."* Jesus does not say that we are not to bother about the speck in our brother's eye, that we are never under any circumstances to pass judgment upon our neighbor. He says we are to be concerned first of all about ourselves. We are to judge ourselves before we judge others. We are not able to criticize or judge others helpfully and constructively until we do first criticize ourselves. If we do cast out our own beam then we will be charitable and sympathetic and clear-sighted in regard to our neighbor.

This is a truth of very wide application and a very important one for our own day. I am not in a position to pass helpful judgment on my children's conduct and to give them constructive help in overcoming their faults unless I recognize my own weakness under temptation, and unless I see my own faults which it may be are partly responsible for theirs. The mistress who resents her maid's impudence will do well to examine her own conduct to consider whether she herself is without blame. Only when she has examined critically her own bearing toward her maid is she in a position to help the latter overcome her fault.

We judge Negroes sometimes (and properly so) for their low standard of sexual morality. But we need to remember how difficult it was for them to retain their marital ties during the days of slavery, how difficult it is for them to maintain the highest moral standards in the environment in which even now they are forced to live. Some years ago a careful study was made of Negro living conditions in one of our Southern cities. The survey showed that the Negroes had a higher crime rate and a higher venereal rate than the whites, which was what everyone expected. But it also showed that the homes in which many Negroes were forced to live were a disgrace to the city. The Negroes paid higher rents for their homes than did the whites for homes of comparable value. But they lacked many facilities not only for comfort but also for decency. Adolescent boys and girls were forced to dress and undress in the same room. And in one of the most crowded sections where the crime rate was highest, no provision whatsoever was made for the recreation of these same adolescents. These were conditions for which the white people of that city were responsible. They were not in a position to judge the conduct of the Negroes in their own city fairly, helpfully, constructively, until they first recognized their own failure. Fortunately they did recognize their responsibility—in part, at least—and conditions today are greatly improved.

I talked once with a man whose business it is to deal with organized labor in a large and important industry. This man, who has established an enviable record in his work, confessed frankly that many of the faults of labor are to be attributed to management's attitude toward labor in the past and now, and this is one of the secrets of his success as a human relations expert. Management must recognize its own faults if it is to get along well with labor, and labor must recognize its faults if it is to receive maximum co-operation from management.

An American sergeant, serving with the American occupation forces in Belgium, wrote a few months after the German collapse as follows: "Before we condemn so sanctimoniously *all* Germans, before we assign a mass guilt for the concentration camp horrors, for German crimes, before we prostitute our faculties of discrimination completely, let us ask ourselves how much we know about a few things in our own fair land: What do we know of conditions in our Japanese-American relocation centers; in many of our prisons; in our police third-degree bouts; in the Georgia chain gangs; how much do we know about what the Negro puts up with every day of his life, what the Jehovah's Witnesses and the conscientious objector had to suffer?

"Our native horrors scarcely compare with the worst of the crimes committed by Germans, yet we have plenty of our own atrocities. And how many times have we not trusted to our own administrators to adjudicate cases where injustice has been done? What we ourselves have done, many a German has done also. If the bulk of Americans are so wise and wide-awake that they know about the conditions of the minority groups and institutions mentioned, if they can say they have themselves *fought* against these inequities and not by-passed them, have fought terrorism, racial discrimination, and the enemies of liberty—then with some justice they can condemn Germans collectively for the nigh incredible inhumanities recently publicized. But if most of us have not fought injustice on American soil, have not fought fascism with the American label—is there not need of more humility, sympathy, and understanding of others?" [39]

We cannot judge the people of any other land fairly until we have first judged ourselves.

"First take the log out of your own eye, and then you will see clearly to take the speck out of your brother's eye"—this is Jesus' first rule for personal religious living, for achieving the righteousness of the Kingdom, but it is only the first.

2. "WHATEVER YOU WISH THAT MEN WOULD DO TO YOU, DO SO TO THEM." Matthew 7:12

So far as we know, this was an absolutely new summary of man's duty to his fellow men. Other teachers, both Jewish and pagan, had said things resembling it. Confucius put it in negative form, as did the great Jewish rabbi, Hillel. Aristotle said we should bear ourselves toward others as we would desire that they should bear themselves toward us. But no one made the rule so comprehensive, so sweeping, as Jesus—to do to all men, not merely to our friends, what we would have them do unto us.

Of course this rule does not sum up the whole of Christian ethics. It does not give the answer to every problem. Men determined to live by the Golden Rule would still make mistakes. With the best intentions in the world they would continue to do foolish and harmful things through sheer inability to understand the problem they were trying to solve. Good will is no substitute for wisdom, and many of our problems are extremely complicated. But with all this the Golden Rule offers a simple rule-of-thumb which throws light on every relation of life, and which can be applied quickly to every situation. It means not only that we shall be courteous, helpful, and just to all men as we desire them to be courteous, helpful, and just to us, but also that we shall endeavor to put ourselves sympathetically and imaginatively in their place and to do to them as we would have them do to us if we were in their position and they in ours. If husbands and wives would thus practice the Golden Rule most domestic problems would disappear. If employer and employee would thus sympathetically put themselves in the position of the other, industrial problems would not prove insurmountable. If white people would put themselves in the place of the Negroes and try to see things from their point of view, if Negroes would follow the reverse procedure, and if both would begin to do what they would like the other to do if they were in their place, racial tensions would begin to resolve. What does it mean to a Negro child to discover for the first time that people regard him with contempt because his skin is black? What anguish do we cause Negro fathers and mothers when we deny their sons and daughters opportunities which we claim for our own as a matter of course! What humiliations do we press daily upon millions of sensitive souls in the abuses which attend our practice of segregation!

Put yourself in the place of the Negro. Imagine, for example, what would happen if, tomorrow morning, you would awaken from your sleep and find that you and all your family had become black. You would probably have to move, and that very quickly, into a different and a very much less desirable neighborhood. You might be able to carry on your profession or to continue your business, but under far humbler circumstances. You would not find the same intellectual and social companionship—a few men and women, perhaps, whose minds had been broadened and enriched, but only a few, would come within the circle to which you were confined. You would have to abandon many of your favorite sports, and to choose a different type of vacation. In many cities, you and your wife would be forced to make your way the back of the bus, and would be subject to daily humiliations and indignities from certain types of people which you would not dare to resent openly. If any altercation arose, and the matter was taken to the police court, the chances are that your word would not be taken against those of your erstwhile neighbors or even the street loafer who happened to be white. You would find it more difficult to educate your children, and if and when their education was achieved they would find it difficult to secure a position to which their culture and their education entitled them. Your daughter could always find a job in domestic service, if she was willing to eat in the kitchen, and if she could remain humble and courteous no matter how demanding or how abusive her mistress might become. If you and your family drove for a summer outing you would have to be satisfied with inferior accommodations. If you were injured in an automobile accident, you could not expect to be taken to the nearest hospital, for it would probably be for whites only, but a white doctor would give you emergency relief in a Negro home, and an ambulance would finally come to convey you to the nearest hospital that was willing to receive Negro patients. Even your old church would not welcome you. It might seat you in an inconspicuous corner. But only a few mature Christians would sit down with you at a table even when you were on the business of your and their common Lord.

Put yourself in the Negro's place. And then do to him as you would have him do to you if you were in his position. This is Jesus' very simple but very profound solution for the race problem. And Negroes, of course, must put themselves in the place of their white neighbors and realize how difficult it is for even the best intentioned to break with the traditions and the practices of their group. A hotel, for example, which extends its services to Negro patrons may face the withdrawal of the white patrons on whom it is dependent for support. The Golden Rule is applicable to both Negroes and whites. It may not solve our race problem, but it points the way out.

What about international relations? Does the Golden Rule have any application here? Undoubtedly it does. Dr. MacIver,

professor of Political Science in Columbia University, puts it thus:
"In war the principle must be: Do to the enemy as he would do
to you, and do it first. In peace, the eternal first principle of
ethics stands as the condition of well-being, in the relations alike
of man and of peoples, do to others as you would have others do
to you." [40]

"No treaty or contract can bind," says Pitirim A. Sorokin, "if
the parties concerned are cynical, nihilistic, free from the categori-
cal imperative of prescribed norms and values. If not the sublim-
est norms of the Sermon on the Mount, which transcend the
power of most mortals, then an approximation to these norms in
the form of the imperatives, 'Do not do to other groups what
you would not like to have done to your group,' and 'Do to other
groups what you would like to have done to your group,' must be
promulgated and deeply grafted into the heart and soul, into the
mind and actual conduct of all human beings and of all states,
nations, people and their leaders, before a lasting peace can
readily be established . . . leaving the details out of consideration
. . . the essence of the proposition remains perfectly clear. All
plans for lasting peace which disregard it or view it as a mere detail or pious wish are doomed to failure: they fool even their
authors. For without this minimum of moral organization no lasting peace is possible." [41]

"Whatever you wish that men would do to you, do so to them."
This is the second rule by which we measure up to the righteousness of the Kingdom, and through which we may secure God's
blessing for ourselves and society, but there is a third which goes
beyond self, beyond our neighbor even, and looks unto God.

3. "Ask . . . Seek . . . Knock." Matthew 7:7-11

Jesus is speaking here about prayer. But the prayer that he
encourages includes more than mere words. It means not only to
ask (petition) but also to seek (which implies intellectual effort)
and to knock (which involves physical exertion). There are three
ways in which a man can co-operate with God, says Dr. Fosdick
in his excellent little book on *The Meaning of Prayer*—thought,

work, and prayer. There are some things which God can do through a man only as he thinks, there are some things which God can do only as he works, and there are some things which God can do only as he prays; but no one of these three can ever quite take the place of the other two. This is a very helpful analysis, and very true. But Jesus' words suggest that thought, work, and prayer are inextricably bound together—if we are to co-operate with God, or if God is to work through us for our highest good. We must ask and we must seek and we must knock, all at the same time. It will not do much good, for example, to pray (i.e., ask) for a peaceful world, if we are not willing to give hard and serious thought to how this may be accomplished, and if we are not willing to knock (i. e., work) that doors may be opened and obstacles removed. In the Greek, the tenses used indicate continuous and repeated effort: Keep on asking and it will be given you; keep on seeking and you will find; keep on knocking and it will be opened to you.

How are we to understand Jesus' promise? Does it apply to material blessings or to spiritual blessings? If we study the words in their context we shall probably agree that the promise applies primarily to the latter. Jesus has been talking about the Kingdom of God—the blessings of the Kingdom and the righteousness of the Kingdom. Now he tells us how we may obtain them: "Ask, and it will be given you; seek, and you will find; knock, and it will be opened to you." Luke in a parallel passage indicates that this is his conception, for he quotes Jesus as explaining his promise in these words: "If you then, who are evil, know how to give good gifts to your children, how much more will the heavenly Father give the *Holy Spirit* to those who ask him?" (Luke 11:13.)

The promise applies, then, first of all to moral and spiritual values, and here it is absolutely true. If we ask sincerely enough, seek zealously enough, and knock persistently enough, keep on asking, keep on seeking, and keep on knocking, we will receive, we will find, ways will be opened to us.

In regard to material things, the promise also tends to be true. But there is no assurance that we shall obtain the things for

which we ask. And we can be thankful that this is so. I woul
be afraid to pray if I did not know that God is wiser than I, th
he answers me not necessarily as I have asked but according to h
infinite wisdom and love. That, applied to material things, is th
promise here: Ask, and you will receive not necessarily what yo
ask, but what is best.

Goodspeed translates Jesus' words in verse 8: "For it is alwa
the one who asks who receives, and the one who searches wh
finds, and the one who knocks to whom the door opens." That
true of earthly things—wisdom, wealth, prestige, or power. It
also true of heavenly things. We cannot get the blessings of th
Kingdom or its righteousness unless we ask, seek, and knock.
we keep on asking, keep on seeking, and keep on knocking, w
will receive; for, as Moffatt translates the verse: "Everyone wh
asks receives, the seeker finds, the door is opened to anyone wh
knocks."

The argument in verses 9-11 is from the less to the greater. W
give good gifts to our children. How much more will our heaven
Father give good gifts to those who ask him? But why does Jest
speak of a stone for a loaf and a serpent for a fish? I think it
because so often God seems to give us a stone. We pray for healt
and health never comes; we pray for the life of some loved or
and death arrives instead. We ask for bread and it seems
though God has given us a stone. But we know that this cann
be the case. We trust God and know that some day we shall kno
even as now we are fully known.

III

The Summons to the Kingdom

Matthew 7:13-27

THE TWO WAYS

Matthew 7:13-14

13 "Enter by the narrow gate; for the gate is wide and the way is easy, that leads to destruction, and those who enter by it are many. 14 For the gate is narrow and the way is hard, that leads to life, and those who find it are few."

Jesus has described the citizens of the Kingdom. He has explained its righteousness. He turns now to his hearers and invites them to enter the Kingdom by the narrow gate—"narrow" because one can enter only as he is willing to tread the path that Jesus has indicated.

He has a reason for pressing the invitation. There are two ways that a man may tread: the easy way with its wide gate and broad road, which is the popular way; and the difficult way with its narrow gate and hard path which so few are willing to take. The choice between these two roads is an important one, for the broad and easy way leads to destruction; the hard and narrow way leads to life (for nations as well as individuals).

THE TWO DANGERS

Matthew 7:15-23

15 "Beware of false prophets, who come to you in sheep's clothing but inwardly are ravenous wolves. 16 You will know them by their fruits. Are grapes gathered from thorns, or figs from thistles? 17 So, every sound tree bears good fruit, but the

bad tree bears evil fruit. [18]A sound tree cannot bear evil fruit, nor can a bad tree bear good fruit. [19]Every tree that does not bear good fruit is cut down and thrown into the fire. [20]Thus you will know them by their fruits.

[21] "Not every one who says to me, 'Lord, Lord,' shall enter the kingdom of heaven, but he who does the will of my Father who is in heaven. [22]On that day many will say to me, 'Lord, Lord, did we not prophesy in your name, and cast out demons in your name, and do many mighty works in your name?' [23]And then will I declare to them, 'I never knew you; depart from me, you evildoers.' "

Even if a man determines to follow the way that leads to life there are dangers against which he needs to be warned.

1. THE DANGER OF FALSE TEACHERS. Matthew 7:15-20

As Jesus puts it: *"Beware of false prophets* [not men who foretell the future only, but all men who claim to speak for God]; *they come to you with the garb of sheep but at heart they are ravenous wolves. You will know them by their fruit."* (Moffatt.) These words of Jesus are somewhat surprising. We might have expected him to say, You will know them by their beliefs, their interpretations of texts, their fidelity to creeds. But not so. He said we could distinguish the false prophet from the true one by his fruit, by the temper he displays, by the spirit he manifests, by the character that he reveals, by the deeds he does, by the life he lives. A man who prides himself on his orthodoxy, but who is uncharitable and bitter and hard, is dangerous, a wolf in sheep's clothing. He is dangerous, because we may be infected by his spirit. We may conclude that we are on the right road because we have the "true" doctrine even though our souls are poisoned by hate. Let us not forget, "You will know them by their fruits."

Jesus' words apply to all men and to all institutions, but especially to teachers, to preachers, to statesmen, to political guides and educational pundits, to all who seek to lead and persuade their fellow men. The men and their theories can be judged by their fruit—if that is bad, the tree itself, however beautiful it may appear, is rotten.

The words also have a reverse application that is not unimportant. We cannot have a better world until we have better men. the only way to get a good life is to get a good heart. To improve the fruit we must first improve the tree.

2. THE DANGER OF A FALSE PROFESSION. Matthew 7:21-23

The test that Jesus gives us whereby we may know false teachers prepares us for the second danger that we face, the danger of a false profession. *"Not every one who says to me, 'Lord, Lord,'"* says Jesus, *"shall enter the kingdom of heaven, but he who does the will of my Father who is in heaven."* We, too, shall be tested not by the words of our lips but by the fruit of our lives. It may be that we are teachers or preachers or workers in the church, that we have been successful in the work that we are doing for the Master, but that is not the fruit of which he is speaking. *"On that day many will say to to me, 'Lord, Lord, did we not prophesy [preach, teach] in your name, and cast out demons in your name, and do many mighty works in your name?' And then will I declare to them, 'I never knew you; depart from me, you evil doers.'"* Someone has suggested that to call Jesus "Lord" is orthodoxy; to call him "Lord, Lord" is piety; but to call him "Lord, Lord" and not do the things which he has commanded is blasphemy.

There are other dangers that we face as we seek to follow Christ, but these are two of the most subtle, because their victims are so often blinded. There is no error so dangerous, because there is none so hard to detect, as the common delusion that doctrine can take the place of deeds, that orthodoxy (right beliefs) can substitute for orthopraxis (right conduct).

THE TWO FOUNDATIONS

Matthew 7:24-27

24 "Every one then who hears these words of mine and does them will be like a wise man who built his house upon the rock; 25 and the rain fell, and the floods came, and the winds blew and beat upon that house, but it did not fall, because it

had been founded on the rock. [26] And every one who hears
these words of mine and does not do them will be like a foolish man who built his house upon the sand; [27] and the rain
fell, and the floods came, and the winds blew and beat against
that house, and it fell; and great was the fall of it."

Jesus has been speaking of the two ways and the dangers en-
countered thereon. In the final paragraph he changes the figure
and compares man's life to a building. But there are two types
of buildings.

The wise man (more exactly, the prudent or sensible man)
builds his house upon the rock; the foolish man builds his house
upon the sand. The figure is based on conditions in Palestine. "In
lands where houses have to be built on the mountainside, it is
usually necessary to build out a solid revetment, which should be
made continuous with the native rock. If a careless or dishonest
builder is content to run a wall across and to fill in the space with
earth instead of with solid bricks, a heavy rainstorm may wash
the earth away and leave the house to fall." [42] But in any land a
prudent builder will be careful about his foundation.

On both houses in Jesus' figure the rains descended, and in
consequence the rivers came (mountain torrents rushing down
the ravine). In the one case the foundation stood firm; in the
other it began to wash away, so that when the winds beat upon it
the building collapsed. "Great was the fall of it," does not mean
that the building was a large one, but that the whole edifice fell,
or fell in, so that the ruin was complete.

Four truths are contained in this familiar parable.

1. All men are building.

> "Isn't it strange
> That princes and kings
> And clowns that caper
> In sawdust rings,
> And common people
> Like you and me
> Are builders for eternity?" [43]

The metaphor, says Plummer, is especially appropriate. "The
man is not pitching a tent for a few hours or at most for a few

ys with the probability of being able to move it in case of
nger, but building a house to dwell in permanently, with cer-
nty that danger must arise sometimes. And that is what we are
ployed upon here; each one is building up his character—
t character which is the one thing which he can take with him,
ich he must take with him into the other world. And the
oice which he has is not between building and not building (he
st build some kind of character) but between building well
d building foolishly."[44] That brings us to the second truth.

2. All men have a choice of foundations. There are innumer-
le philosophies of life which a man may choose. But Jesus nar-
ws the choice drastically. A man must choose whether or not
will build his life on Jesus' words. That is the one choice which
supremely meaningful.

3. All foundations will be tried—tried by the storms of life.
to everyone's life comes sickness, disappointment, death; heavy
ief of one sort or another drives its plowshare deep into the
man heart. As an old Eastern proverb has it, "Every man has
date with adversity and it is a date which adversity never fails
meet." The difference between individuals, says Hastings, is
t the measure of adversity which comes to them (though some
experience more adversity than others), but what they do
th adversity when it appears. In every life, sooner or later, the
ins descend, the winds beat, the floods rise, but for one man
e house of life falls in ruins, while for another it stands secure;
d the difference lies not in the intensity of the storm, but in
e power to withstand.

Storms reveal the quality of one's life. One stands firm under
e strain, another collapses. There have always been men of the
rmer sort: like Milton, for example, who wrote in his blindness,

> "I argue not
> Against Heav'n's hand or will, nor bate a jot
> Of heart or hope; but still bear up and steer
> Right onward."[45]

d there have always been those whose strength proved un-
ual to the strain.

Jesus' words apply to Christians as well as to non-Christians; not only to small characters but also to great; not only to the humblest disciple, but also to apostles. His words apply to the ordinary storms of life, all of those things which try men's characters and reveal the quality of their lives, but undoubtedly he is thinking, too, of that last scene when each character shall meet its supreme test. And that brings us to the final thought.

4. Jesus' words afford the only secure foundation for time or eternity. Note that it is Jesus' words which afford security, and that they afford security only as men hear and obey. (Cf. 7:21.) Trust in Christ as Saviour does not afford a safe foundation for this life or the next, unless it includes loyal submission to him as Lord. Professions are of no avail unless one does the will of God. "These words of mine" refers particularly to the Sermon on the Mount. He that hears *these words* and does not do them will be like a foolish man who built his house upon the sand.

And so the Sermon on the Mount ends—with a warning to men individually, but also, we can be sure, to nations. That becomes clear as we read how Jesus entered Jerusalem for the last time: "And when he drew near and saw the city he wept over it, saying, 'Would that even today you knew the things that make for peace! But now they are hid from your eyes. For the days shall come upon you, when your enemies will cast up a bank about you and surround you, and hem you in on every side, and dash you to the ground, you and your children within you, and they will not leave one stone upon another in you; because you did not know the time of your visitation.'" (Luke 19:41-44. See also Matthew 23: 37-39.)

Notes and Acknowledgments

1. Vladimir G. Simkhovitch, *Toward the Understanding of Jesus*, p. 45. New York: The Macmillan Company. Used by permission.
2. Shailer Matthews, *New Testament Times in Palestine*, p. 237. New York: The Macmillan Company. Used by permission.
3. Arvel Steece, "World Planners," first published in *The Christian Century*, March 20, 1946. Used by permission of the author.
4. Charles Gore, Henry Leighton Goudge, and Alfred Guillaume, editors, *A New Commentary on Holy Scripture*, Part III, p. 137. New York: The Macmillan Company. Used by permission.
5. In this section the author is greatly indebted to the suggestive study, *The Way* by William Pierson Merrill.
6. William Pierson Merrill, *The Way*, p. 24. New York: The Macmillan Company. Used by permission.
7. *Ibid.*
8. *Ibid.*, p. 25.
9. *Ibid.*
10. *Ibid.*, pp. 26-27.
11. *Ibid.*, p. 27.
12. George A. Buttrick, *The Interpreter's Bible*, Vol. VII, p. 285. Nashville: Abingdon Press.
13. Merrill, *op. cit.*, p. 16.
14. *Ibid.*, p. 41.
15. Theodore H. Robinson, *The Gospel of Matthew*, p. 35. New York: Harper & Brothers. Used by permission.
16. Earl L. Douglass in *The Snowden Sunday School Lessons*, 1939, p. 316. New York: The Macmillan Company. Used by permission.
17. Washington Gladden, *Recollections*, p. 147. Boston: Houghton Mifflin Company.
18. *Ibid.*, p. 153.
19. *Ibid.*, pp. 156-157.
20. Paul G. Hutchinson, *From Victory to Peace*, p. 100. Willett Clark and Company. Used by permission..
21. Hallet Abend, *Ramparts of the Pacific*. New York: Doubleday, Doran and Company. Used by permission.
22. Gore *et al.*, *op. cit.*, Part III, p. 140.
23. *Ibid.*
24. Robinson, *op. cit.*, p. 43.
25. Herbert Hoover and Hugh Gibson, *The Problems of Lasting Peace*. New York: Doubleday, Doran and Company. Used by permission.
26. Ernie Pyle, *Brave Men*. New York: Grosset and Dunlap. Used by permission.
27. David Smith, *Commentary on the Four Gospels—Matthew*, pp. 117-118. New York: Harper & Brothers. Used by permission.
28. Harry Emerson Fosdick, *The Meaning of Prayer*, p. 33. New York: Association Press. Used by permission.

29. Merrill, *op. cit.*, p. 107.
30. Adolf Keller, *Christian Europe Today*, p. 200. New York: Harper Brothers. Used by permission.
31. Robinson, *op. cit.*, p. 54.
32. Smith, *op. cit.*, p. 120.
33. Robinson, *op. cit.*, p. 55.
34. Pitirim A. Sorokin, *The Crisis of Our Age*, p. 240. New York: E. P. Dutton and Company. Used by permission.
35. Conrad Noel, *The Life of Jesus*. New York: Simon and Schuster. Used permission.
36. *Information Service*, June 16, 1945, reviewing *Education and the Promise of America* by George Counts.
37. *A Message to the Churches* from The National Study Conference on Churches and on Just and Durable Peace.
38. *The New Republic*, June 25, 1945. Used by permission.
39. *Ibid.*, July 16, 1945.
40. R. M. MacIver, *Towards an Abiding Peace*, p. 44. New York: The Macmillan Company. Used by permission.
41. Pitirim A. Sorokin, *Russia and the United States*, pp. 236-237. New York: E. P. Dutton and Company. Used by permission.
42. Robinson, *op. cit.*, p. 66.
43. Margaret Slattery, "One in Seven."
44. Alfred Plummer, *An Exegetical Commentary on the Gospel According to Saint Matthew*, p. 119. New York: Charles Scribner's Sons. Used by permission.
45. John Milton, "Sonnet XXII."